SheriLynn's story will inspire you to dream bigger than you've allowed yourself to for a long time. If you're looking for a fresh dose of encouragement, look no further.

LISA BEVERE
New York Times Bestselling Author

SheriLynn's book is a living example of how God does exceedingly abundantly more than we could ever ask or imagine when we allow His powerful hand to lead us to His path for us! You will be lead into the world of "how to" live a life worthy of the calling you have received as you weave through SheriLynn's personal life story of overcoming obstacles. She shares through total transparency how to embrace life through the eyes and heart of faith. This book can literally be a launching pad for you to begin living the life of all you ever dreamt possible.

CINDY PENTECOST
Co-Founder of It Works!

SheriLynn's debut book is such a remarkable collection of truths about what we are capable of achieving in life. Her own story is a testament to the power of vision and hard work, and her words will inspire anyone to reignite their own dreams.

STELLA REED
Lead Pastor & Executive Director, Dream Center NYC

You Can Do Hard Things

You Can Do Hard Things

how to ditch the excuses
& achieve your dreams

SHERILYNN ALCALA

Copyright © 2020 by SheriLynn Alcala.

All rights reserved. No part of this publication may be reproduced, distributed, or transmitted in any form or by any means, including photocopying, recording, or other electronic or mechanical methods, without the prior written permission of the publisher, except in the case of brief quotations embodied in critical reviews and certain other noncommercial uses permitted by copyright law. For permission requests, write to the publisher at the address below.

Fedd Books
P.O. Box 341973
Austin, TX 78734

www.thefeddagency.com

Published in association with The Fedd Agency, Inc., a literary agency.

Unless otherwise noted, all scripture quotations are taken from the Holy Bible, New International Version®, NIV®. Copyright © 1973, 1978, 1984, 2011 by Biblica, Inc.™ Used by permission of Zondervan. All rights reserved worldwide. www.zondervan.com The "NIV" and "New International Version" are trademarks registered in the United States Patent and Trademark Office by Biblica, Inc.™

Scripture quotations marked (ESV) are taken from the ESV® Bible (The Holy Bible, English Standard Version®), copyright © 2001 by Crossway, a publishing ministry of Good News Publishers. Used by permission. All rights reserved.

Scripture quotations marked (AMP) are taken from the Amplified Bible Copyright © 1954, 1958, 1962, 1964, 1965, 1987 by The Lockman Foundation, La Habra, CA. All rights reserved. Used by Permission. www.lockman.org.

Scripture quotations marked (KJV) are taken from the King James Version of the Bible.

Scripture quotations marked (MEV) are taken from the Modern English Version. Copyright © 2014 by Military Bible Association. Used by permission. All rights reserved.

Scripture quotations marked (CSB) are taken from the Christian Standard Bible. Copyright © 2017 by Holman Bible Publishers. Used by permission. Christian Standard Bible®, and CSB® are federally registered trademarks of Holman Bible Publishers, all rights reserved.

Scripture quotations marked (NKJV) are taken from the New King James Version®. Copyright © 1982 by Thomas Nelson. Used by permission. All rights reserved.

Scripture quotations marked (NLT) are taken from the Holy Bible, New Living Translation, copyright ©1996, 2004, 2015 by Tyndale House Foundation. Used by permission of Tyndale House Publishers, Inc., Carol Stream, Illinois 60188. All rights reserved.

Scripture quotations marked (ERV) are taken from the Easy-To-Read Version. Copyright © 2006 by Bible League International.

ISBN: 978-1-949784-39-8
eISBN: 978-1-949784-40-4

Library of Congress Control Number: 2020903562

Printed in the United States of America

First Edition 15 14 13 12 11 / 10 9 8 7 6 5 4 3 2

I want to dedicate this book to my daughters, Josse & Jewel. Because of you two, I found the courage to dream again. My prayer is that you girls would grow up knowing that you truly can do all things through Christ who gives you strength! I cannot wait to sit front row and watch you girls change your world. Mommy will always be your biggest cheerleader.

TABLE OF CONTENTS

Introduction: The Back Burner 11

1. You Can Just Start 23
2. You Can Find Your Why 37
3. You Can Fail Forward 51
4. You Can Have Vision 65
5. You Can Work For It 87
6. You Can Release Your Past 109
7. You Can Be Enough 127
8. You Can Tune Out the Critics 145
9. You Can Find Your People 159
10. You Can Say No 175
11. You Can Have It All 187
12. You Can Show Up 203

Conclusion: You Can Do Hard Things 219
Acknowledgments 225
Endnotes 227

Introduction

THE BACK BURNER

When I was little, my mind was full of dreams. On any given day, I dreamed of being a professional dancer, a veterinarian, a lawyer, the first female president—sometimes of being all of those things at once. I had a bin in our playroom full of dress-up clothes, so you never knew if I was going to be a Hollywood actress or an extraordinary doctor who earned her third Nobel Prize. I was unashamed, ready, and willing to tell anyone who asked about my dreams what I wanted to be. And I honestly believed I could achieve any of them.

Childhood dreams are so pure and uninhibited, and for the most part, people encourage imagination and exploration. When we are young, no one feels the need to temper our dreams. Then somewhere between childhood and adulthood, people begin to question our dreams more. People begin to expect pragmatic, reasonable, and logical dreams rather than imaginative, visionary, and bold ones. Somewhere along the way, we are told to shrink back.

YOU CAN DO HARD THINGS

We begin to buy into this idea that we have to be realistic and practical. You can either be logical or visionary. You can either be all business, or you can be a daydreamer—there's no room for both. It is as though there is this invisible box that we are all expected to fit inside. As long as your dreams fit inside the box, things will be okay, but heaven forbid you dare to dream beyond the box. For some reason, all of a sudden, we begin to feel the need to be "realists." We look at our dreams in such a practical manner that we unknowingly take our dreams and squish them in that box.

We begin to question ourselves, our dreams, and our capabilities. We start to only attempt things that we know we will be able to do. I don't think we ever truly stop dreaming, but most of us just begin to pay less and less attention to our dreams. We begin to downsize them, often to the point where they disappear altogether.

As women, we have a tendency to put our dreams on the back burner. You know how we all have a favorite stovetop burner that we always prefer to use? And there is one that we never use for whatever reason? Similar to those stovetop burners, we have responsibilities that we tend to put first and dreams that we tend to suppress or ignore. More often than not, women have a plethora of things in the forefront of their minds: spouse, kids, all of their activities, school, work, friends, laundry, grocery shopping, random things that we've said yes to but can't for the life of us remember why. And then we realize there is no more room for our dreams, so we place them on the

INTRODUCTION

back burner—the one we never look at and often forget about. We pay less attention to our dreams in order to help fulfill the dreams of those around us. Whether it's because we've been told we can't achieve our dreams, or that we can't be too successful, or because we naturally help others more than we help ourselves, chasing after dreams as women isn't exactly easy or encouraged. Our tendencies toward self-doubt, insecurity, and comparison often hold us back and keep us stuck in our limitations. We get squished back into that invisible box of what's reasonable, acceptable, and necessary with no room for anything extra.

Time seems to be the culprit. There are not enough hours in the day for dreams, right? If we look a little deeper, we will see that our priorities are actually what need adjusting. How many of us have thought: *I will pursue that when my babies are no longer little and in diapers. I will start that project when my children are in school. I will get to it when my kids are more self-sufficient. Once I get them all off to college, the time will be perfect.*

Or maybe your narrative sounds more like: *I will begin when work slows down. I will attempt to start when they hire someone else to take the load off of me. When I am able to quit this job, I can really pursue my true dream.* We sit back and let these words play on repeat in our minds. We do all the other things and wait for the perfect timing. We wait for the situation to be less risky. We are waiting for the laundry to be folded and the kids to be potty-trained, for the holidays to end and for January to roll around so we can make some resolutions. We are waiting for the front burners of our mind to be empty before we ever think to turn on the back burner and let our dreams come back to life again. The problem is—those front burner things don't ever fully go away. So, we've got some work to do. How can we begin to balance and prioritize our responsibilities *and* those big dreams in our hearts?

This world is full of women with so many visions, goals, and dreams bottled up inside of them. But far too many are scared to take the steps and put in the work to see their dreams come to life. Is it easy to accomplish your dreams? No, it's not. In fact, it will require work, dedication, and consistency. But as women, we have a strength and persistence that is unmatched. We have to take our dedication that is usually reserved for others and put it toward ourselves and our dreams. Girls, it isn't arrogant or selfish to believe in yourself and believe you can achieve your dreams. If anything, I think many of us lack this kind of confidence. We doubt ourselves, we count ourselves out, we think, "That's for her but not me." That is nonsense. Whatever your dream or goal is, I want to help you go from shrugging it off to multiplying it by ten and visualizing yourself crushing it! Over the coming chapters, I want to equip you with some really practical

> **We have to take our dedication that is usually reserved for others and put it toward ourselves and our dreams.**

INTRODUCTION

ways to take steps towards bringing those big dreams to life.

Let me tell you, though, as you start to pursue your dream, it will feel as though everything and everyone is out to stop you. You, for one, will get in your own way. There will be so many excuses that will rear their ugly heads. Insecurity, self-doubt, and fear of stepping into the unknown will come at you. We can't forget the mile-long list of "What Ifs" that will go through your head and attempt to trip you up. Then there is your past. Your past will try to haunt you, reminding you of all the times you failed before. All of a sudden, you begin to second guess if you are even worthy of your dream.

In order to get to the actual "achieve your dreams" part of life, we've got to first identify the kinds of excuses we make. I want to walk through each excuse listed above and demonstrate how these things don't have the final word in our lives. The only small problem? We've repeated these excuses to ourselves so much that we actually have come to believe them. Sister, I want to confront these excuses with the truth. As we begin to ditch our excuses and replant truth in our hearts, we will grow in confidence, in boldness, and in character. I want to not just tell you the truth, but help you truly believe that you can do hard things. You can see that dream in your heart become your real life.

I am a dreamer. Like I told you, I have been since I was a little girl. But even as a self-proclaimed dreamer, every time I discover a new dream, my mind starts to wander toward thoughts of doubt and fear. It seems impossible, daunting, and even crazy at first. Each time I come to this crossroads in my heart and mind, I have the choice to ignore the dream or to tackle it. Retreating is so much easier than actually going into battle to fight for that dream. Most of us tend to dismiss the dream rather than pursue it because we don't like to make waves or press into any sort of discomfort. Sometimes the best thing you can do for yourself, and the world, is make waves. Sometimes the bravest and best thing you can do is dream anyway—dream despite the excuses, insecurity, fear, criticism, and doubt. Dream because uninhibited dreams can change the world—especially your world!

I have not always been so sure of myself, though. My dream-first mentality has emerged after years of hard work and discipline. Let me tell you how things were when this all started. My husband, John, and I had been married for about a year, and we were living in Midland, Texas. Things were tight financially. I was in college and working as an assistant to a family. I also taught dance classes, and John worked for a cell phone company and was on staff at a church. Things were good. Sure, we could have had some more wiggle room in our finances, but I didn't dare complain. When dreams would pop into my head, I would quickly dismiss them. I had a good life, better than so many others, so who was I to dare

> **Sometimes the best thing you can do for yourself, and the world, is make waves.**

INTRODUCTION

dream bigger? I thought it was selfish to dream of a larger ministry, a bigger home, and more income. I thought dreaming of more meant I was not content with what I had right then. But why would it be selfish to dream bigger? Even within ministry, why is it bad to dream of impacting even more people for Jesus? It's not! But back then, I often felt guilty enlarging my vision. As quick as a dream entered my heart, I would just as soon scale back.

In that first year of marriage, our very first apartment was only 500 square feet. We loved it, but it was a bit difficult trying to cram in twenty young adults when they all came over to watch American Idol. Because we ran the young adults' ministry, the hang outs were always at our home. I told the Lord that if He blessed us with a house, we would use it for His glory and the doors would always be open. Yes, I was thankful for our apartment, but I had to remind myself it was okay to dream of more. I dreamed of owning a home, and maybe a year later, we were able to buy our first home. This was my first lesson in learning that you can be grateful and content with what you have but still dream bigger.

Still, other dreams in my heart started to shrink again when kids came along. After having my second daughter, life felt overwhelming for me. Having two babies under two years old, both in diapers at the same time, was nothing like I imagined. My Type-A, OCD self struggled. My always-clean house was, more often than not, filled with baby toys, crushed cheerios, and piles of laundry that had been waiting to be done for well over a week. If I am going to be completely honest, my husband would run out of clean underwear and have to start a load of laundry at 10:00 p.m. almost weekly because I couldn't stay on top of the mounting pile. I felt, as so many mothers do, that I was hanging on by a thread and at any moment it was going to snap.

Somewhere in all this, I had started a blog that, at one point, I hoped would really be something special. During this season as a new mom, the blog was no longer a priority. The dreams I had for impacting other women through writing began to fade. Even the speaking engagements I had once started taking at different women's ministry events became less frequent and then came to a complete halt. Suddenly, those other things outside of keeping my home running began to seem selfish. They were my dreams, but right now, I couldn't even keep up with these two baby girls and my household. So, I let go and gave up. And isn't it funny that we are often the first ones to talk ourselves out of our dreams?

Since those early days of marriage and motherhood, I have learned to dream of more for myself and my family. I have seen many of those dreams come true. Although our homes have changed and grown, we have always made sure to have open doors. Even now, when people don't have somewhere to eat for Thanksgiving they are welcome here. (We had thirty-five people eat with us last year!) I am blessed that my current home has a spacious office, and I get to work from home and be with my babies while pouring into, empowering, and speaking to women

INTRODUCTION

every day. And I'm happy to report the laundry situation is now under control. How did I get there? Little teeny tiny steps. Incremental changes in my thoughts toward myself. And hard work.

When I began my own business in 2014, I did not dream of being a Top 10 income earner, making millions of dollars, or having a team of thousands. My original dream was to earn eighty dollars a month to put my daughter in dance class. Shoot, if I could make a few hundred dollars a month, that was more than I could have dreamed of earning, and I could maybe go to Target on a whim. Somewhere along the way, that seed of the dream took root, and I decided to let go of fear, release the limitations I was putting on myself, and just go for it. I looked at other top income earners, many of them moms just like me, and I thought: Why not? Why not me? I decided to be bold and audacious. I thought: Why not reach for the stars and see if I could do it? So, I did just that! As a result, I achieved those dreams and then some! After each dream was achieved, I would quickly dream up a new one. Sure, self-doubt and insecurity would creep in each time, but I made the choice to ignore those fears and instead tell myself I can do hard things and I will do them. I can do all things through Christ who gives me strength (Philippians 4:13).

Through pursuing my dreams of being a mom, being financially stable, and starting my own business, I have been able to reach and bless more people than I ever thought possible. The process of pursuing my dreams was hard. It took me breaking down the lies and excuses that would come up when I started to think my goals were not achievable. I had to tackle excuses like "I don't have time," or "My dreams aren't important enough," or "What if I fail?" I had to learn to take my thoughts captive. I would catch the thoughts trying to sabotage my dream in action and replace those thoughts with truths about who I am and what I am capable of accomplishing. And as I grow in this practice of embracing truth, my dreams grow. Through this process, I have learned to not limit myself. I began to really believe Ephesians 3:20-21, "Now to him who is able to do immeasurably more than all we ask or imagine, according to his power that is at work within us, to him be glory . . ." God can do immeasurably more than we could ask or imagine. He is for us and has deposited dreams in our heart that we are designed to fulfill.

When I think about all the beautiful dreams left untouched on the back burner, something inside me starts brewing. If I have figured out some things that have helped me bring those dreams to the forefront of my life, I need to share that with others. I want to remind you, my friends and sisters, that you were made for a purpose, and your dreams, passions, and gifts are all part of that purpose. Pursuing what we are passionate about helps us be the best people we can be. When we are using our gifts and passion to build, create, and execute our dreams, we contribute to the world, we make it a better place, and we make each other better. We can change the world through pursuing our dreams, and who doesn't want to change the world? Not only do you

INTRODUCTION

deserve to chase after your dreams, the world needs you to.

When we let insecurity and self-doubt have free rein in our minds, we let the excuses seem a lot bigger than they actually are. They loom over us and weigh us down. Excuses can be detrimental to becoming the woman you were made to be. You may think that you are being logical or level-headed when you minimize your dreams, but in reality, you are letting excuses keep you from taking the proper steps to achieve your dreams. In this book, we will look at these common excuses that stop women from going after their dreams, then we will break them down and replace them with the truths about who we are and what we are capable of achieving.

> **When we embrace the truths of who we are, we begin dreaming again.**

We can't go back to the unhindered and unchallenged dreams of our youth, but we can take the experience, truth, and unshakable identities that we do have, and we can choose to dream anyway. I want you to walk away from these pages knowing and believing you can do hard things. When we choose to dream despite all the obstacles that come our way, we develop a strength that is incomparable. When we kick excuses to the curb, we stop limiting ourselves. When we embrace the truths of who we are, we begin dreaming again.

Chapter 1

YOU CAN JUST START

> **THE EXCUSE:**
> It's not the right time.

I have so much going on right now and so many other responsibilities. Sure, I have goals and dreams, but now is not the time to pursue them. When things settle or slow down, I'll start pursuing my dream, but the circumstances just aren't right.

I got married my sophomore year of college. My husband, John, and I were twenty-two years old and broke. Early in our marriage, I can clearly remember feeling stuck, even feeling I had settled for less in my life. After we graduated, we were living this paycheck-to-paycheck life of survival. The vision I had once had for my life was slowly fading. I once imagined a life free of financial stress and no debt, having children, going on family vacations, owning a spacious home where we could entertain family and friends, being able to give abundantly to our church and to missions, and going to the store without needing to look for all the deals and coupons. Instead, I was having to calculate each item I was putting into my shopping cart every time I went to the store.

John and I had been married maybe three years when we moved from Midland, Texas to Dallas, Texas to help launch a church plant. John was taking a 40-percent pay cut with his new job in Dallas, and there really wasn't a whole lot to cut to begin with. We found ourselves house poor, trying hard to keep our heads above water and not go into debt. The new norm was us sharing an entrée at a restaurant and ordering water, even if it meant still being hungry after dinner.

John had a 2001 Toyota 4-Runner with 200,000 miles on it, and shortly after our move, it began having mechanical issues. All of a sudden, when you would press the gas pedal, it would not accelerate. You had to quickly pump the gas a few times to get the car to go. This was especially scary when you were trying to make a turn into an intersection with oncoming traffic headed your way. We couldn't afford to have it fixed, so John drove it anyways. He even had to commute thirty miles each way to work in this junker. It was honestly terrifying, but this was our reality.

There were lots of arguments about finances. Usually, these conversations had to do with me overspending and not sticking to the budget John set. I hated the stress this put on our marriage, especially the additional stress it put on John as the primary breadwinner. I would lay in bed at night and wonder if this was just the way life was. We held

JUST START

our breath until February each year because that was when John's company would give out bonuses. Those bonuses were our saving grace to get us through each year. I had dreamed up such a different life, but I was not quite sure how to make my current situation ever look like my dreams.

A couple months after we moved to Dallas, I found out I was pregnant with our second child. I am not going to lie: as excited as we were, there was some uncertainty. This would be another stressor on the budget. Before our first daughter was even one year old, we were already expecting another baby girl; our family kept growing, but our finances had not changed.

I remember thinking: This is how life is going to be forever—stressed about every bill, every trip to the grocery store, every weird noise that my car makes. I felt like there was no way for things to get better. John couldn't make more money than he was making, and I had chosen to stay home with our daughters. This was life. I would tell myself I needed to be thankful things weren't worse. Even with our difficulties, we were more fortunate than so many others, and I just needed to accept the way things were. I was settling with the hand I thought we were dealt. Hear me out: I am not for one minute saying that we shouldn't live a life of gratitude and thankfulness. We do need to be thankful for everything big and small, seen and unseen in our life. I want to be content, but that does not mean that I have to settle. We serve a big, big God. And I believe if we are faithful with the small, He will trust us with more.

One day, I decided I was sick of living the way we

were living. John and I were two adults who both did what we were "supposed to do." We went to college, worked hard, got our degrees. Yet we were living a life so far from the "American Dream" I had imagined. We may have looked picture-perfect on the outside, but inside the four walls of our home, we were struggling to pay the mortgage each month, let alone do anything else. I quickly learned an important lesson: the narrative that we are sold isn't usually the one that we find ourselves in.

I knew I wanted to stay home with my two young girls, and I wanted a way of earning income that would allow me to do that. I wanted that vision to come to life. Even though everything indicated that this wasn't the right time to start something, I couldn't shake this longing. So, I decided I was going to start a home-based business. I had no clue what I was doing or what to do, but there was something tugging at my heart. I knew just sitting there wishing for my circumstances to change wasn't going to cut it! I remembered Deuteronomy 28:8 "The LORD will command the blessing upon you in your barns and in all that you put your hand to . . . " (NASB).

> **The narrative that we are sold isn't usually the one that we find ourselves in.**

When I read Deuteronomy 28:8, I knew the Lord was saying to me that He would bless what I put my hands to. But take note: putting my hands to something is an action. It requires getting up and starting something. It requires pushing past all the excuses and taking the first steps. God put this new dream in my heart, and I finally realized that I could pursue multiple dreams at once. Starting a business didn't mean I had stopped pursuing and living my dream of being a mom—I could do both. Most of the time, we can do more things than we think we can; we just have to be willing to make the decision and show up to work for it.

I get it, it is hard to dream when you feel stuck and you don't see a way out of your circumstances. It is in these seasons of feeling stuck when you have to decide if you are going to just sit back and settle or muster up the courage to put on your big girl panties and do something. Will you have the courage to say, "No way. I refuse to let my current situation or circumstances dictate my future. I may not be able to see how things are going to change yet, but I am determined to fight for that change"? How things look today does not mean that they have to look this way tomorrow. You have a choice in the matter.

I have a feeling a lot of you reading this want to start something. You have a dream that tugs at your heart. You want to see those dreams come to life but where do you begin? When do you begin? When there's work, PTA, laundry, dinner, whatever it may be, what is it going to take to start?

***

YOU CAN DO HARD THINGS

We hear the language of "follow your dreams" all too often, but what are we really saying? We might understand the definition of dreaming, but we then need to evaluate the motives of a dream. A dream is a strongly desired goal or purpose. A dream is a goal we have that flexes our creativity and makes us feel more alive, more present. Once we grasp that definition, then we must ask: when is a dream healthy and when is a dream foolish? If following your dream leads you to becoming more of the person you were born to be and doesn't damage or hinder your relationships, then I would say that is a dream worth pursuing.

A dream looks different for us all. Eight years ago, for me a "dream" meant being able to stay home with my babies but not have to struggle paycheck to paycheck. Your dream could be like mine, or maybe your dream is to go back to school and get that degree you always wanted. Maybe you have dream of getting your real estate license or starting your own business. For others, your dream may be to lead a Bible study, run a marathon, or get physically fit.

> **A dream is a goal we have that flexes our creativity and makes us feel more alive, more present.**

Each of us has that strongly desired goal or sense of purpose that we want to take hold of, but we need help to take the first step forward. Proverbs 16:3 says, "Commit to the Lord whatever you do, and he will establish your plans." If you are ever unsure about following your

JUST START

dreams, then I encourage you to commit whatever your dream is to the Lord. You aren't alone in this. You don't have to take the first step alone. God is right alongside you, and He places dreams in your heart that He works with you to fulfill.

Our excuse we're dismantling in this chapter is all about time. *It isn't the right time to pursue my dream. When the time is right, I'll start.* I know for me, many times I held back from going after those dream in my heart because I was waiting for this elusive "right time." Sometimes, we do need to wait for better timing, but I think more often than not, we use that as an excuse. Each time the dream pops back into our thoughts, we hit the snooze button and try to forget about it for a month or two. Have you ever felt yourself do that? You must fight this instinct toward delaying your dreams because circumstances will never be perfect. You can, however, decide to prioritize your dream and make it fit within your circumstances.

Another reason we neglect to pursue our dreams is because we are comfortable. Maybe you make good income and have a good job. Maybe you are a stay-at-home mom, the bills and everything are paid for, and things are okay . . . but you are yearning for more. I don't care how "comfortable" your situation may be; I don't care how filthy rich you might be. If you have a dream in your heart that you aren't pursuing, then this is your wake up call to get out of your comfort zone and do something about it! The world needs you to achieve the dream that is inside of you. Nothing great will ever happen in your comfort zone. You have to continually dream, set new goals, and stretch yourself. You don't ever "arrive." You accomplish a goal or master a skill, and then you set a new goal. If you have found yourself just settling in your comfortable situation, then it is time to get some fresh vision and dream again. Chasing your dreams and continuing to set new goals helps you become the best version of yourself, it helps you realize everything that you are capable of doing as you learn and grow, and it encourages and inspires others to do the same.

Some of us are waiting for the right time, and others are too comfortable to dream, but for some of you, your situation right now is the furthest thing from comfortable. Whether you are living paycheck to paycheck, swimming in debt, or just feeling empty and stuck, you know there is more to this life. Somewhere along the way, you got comfortable in the struggle. I cannot count the number of times I have had women want to join my team but are concerned that they will make too much income and then lose their government assistance. When I hear that, I want to shake these women and wake them up. Sister, do not for one second allow yourself to get comfortable with your struggle. I want you to think beyond where you are now. I want you to not even need assistance. I want to see your circumstances changing so much that you will be the one who is able to assist others. We have to shift our mentality. Stop talking about your struggle, stop being okay in your struggle, and decide to change it.

When my girls were babies, I had a friend take her son

JUST START

to Disney World. Looking at their photos, I could tell you one thing . . . they went all out. They were at the Grand Floridian Disney resort, and my friend was posting photos of her view of the magical castle from her family's hotel room. They were ordering room service and eating at all those fun character breakfasts. When I scrolled through (and maybe even stalked) her photos, I did not have jealousy or even resentment. My thoughts were more along the lines of: "Wow, what a dream vacation. My kids will never ever experience anything like that. No way, no how. That is not something we would ever be able to do." I remember that moment because that was truly a time where I was not letting myself dream. I think I was trying to guard my heart from disappointment so I didn't dare dream of something grand like a Disney World trip, even though that was a place I had dreamed of going as a little girl.

You may be reading this and thinking Disney World seems like a nightmare, and that's fine. But what is your "Disney World trip" that you quickly dismiss and think would be completely impossible to attain? Are you to scared to take that audition because you think you would never get that role? Do you slam down the laptop every time you open it to start your blog because you think no one would want to read it? Do you stay at your dead end job because you don't believe you are capable of starting your own business?

We settle in our uncomfortable lives and try to make ourselves feel better by telling ourselves, "This was the hand I was dealt," and "This is just how life is." WRONG!

That is a big fat lie of the Enemy and is a cop out for many of us. My Bible (and your Bible too) says in John 10:10, "I have come that they may have life, and have it to the full." You were created to thrive, and living "uncomfortably comfortable" is not thriving. I believe the Lord can birth dreams in our heart, but He isn't going to make you go after them. God doesn't force things on us; we have to decide whether or not to go after the desires He's given us.

> **THE TRUTH:**
> To go after our dreams, we have to *just start*.

We must stop thinking life will slow down and that the "right time" will come along someday. To do hard things, we must lean into the mess of right now and let it be part of our story. Even small steps lead to big change.

There is one story in the Bible that I think demonstrates this truth so clearly. In the book of Esther, Esther is chosen by the King Xerxes to be his queen. During the time that she is chosen, King Xerxes' chief minister, Haman, plotted to massacre the Jews throughout the empire. Esther, who was a Jew herself, found out about the edict from her cousin Mordecai. Mordecai told Esther the whole story, including the exact amount of money Haman had promised to pay into the royal treasury for the destruction of the Jews. He also asked

JUST START

her to go to the king to beg for mercy and plead for her people. Can you imagine being in her position and the fear she must have felt?

Then Esther said to Mordecai, "All the king's officials and even the people in the provinces know that anyone who appears before the king in his inner court without being invited is doomed to die unless the king holds out his gold scepter. And the king has not called for me to come to him for thirty days," (Esther 4:11, NLT). Esther was the queen of "It's not the right time." She was rightfully scared to go to the king in her people's time of need. She was fearful that something bad would happen if she stepped forward and spoke up. Esther wanted to wait for the king to approach her; she wanted to wait until the circumstances were just right. Her response is so relatable. *I wasn't invited, so I can't show up.* She was scared to speak up, to use her voice because it might mean rejection, failure, and in her case, death. She was comfortable with where she was and didn't want to cause any waves.

Mordecai replied to Esther's fear with some hard-hitting truth: "Don't think for a moment that because you're in the palace you will escape when all other Jews are killed. If you keep quiet at a time like this, deliverance and relief for the Jews will arise from some other place, but you and your relatives will die. Who knows if perhaps you were made queen for just such a time as this?" (Esther 4:13-14, NLT). I believe this is the truth we often miss: perhaps the positions and circumstances that you are in right now—yes, even the mess of it all—is exactly what equips you to follow after the dreams that have been laying dormant in your heart. Perhaps the position you are in, rather than being a disadvantage or hindrance, is actually the starting line.

Esther then sent this reply to Mordecai: "Go and gather together all the Jews of Susa and fast for me. Do not eat or drink for three days, night or day. My maids and I will do the same. And then, though it is against the law, I will go in to see the king. If I must die, I must die," (Esther 4:16, NLT). Esther's fear and hesitations didn't just disappear, but she pushed past them and bravely took a step forward. Esther then spoke with the king and changed his mind, saving all the Jews in the kingdom. Because of her step forward, despite the possible consequences, she changed the world and saved many lives.

> Perhaps the position you are in, rather than being a disadvantage or hindrance, is actually the starting line.

I am here to tell you, like Mordecai told Esther, "Perhaps you were made for just such a time as this." Don't let fear, comfort, or excuses get in the way of you fulfilling your purpose and your dreams. The circumstances are never going to align perfectly in our minds, but that's where faith comes in. You have to just start. Make time for your dreams, even if it's just a little bit at first! You were created for such a time as this, and I believe that with every fiber in my being. Take that first step!

JUST START

Sometimes the task before us seems daunting—we are standing at the starting line, knowing that there is a whole race ahead of us. We feel uneasy and uncertain, wondering whether we can finish the race. We remember the pain in our knees and how little sleep we got the night before, and we wonder if running this race is a good idea. "Next year . . . ", we think. Though our minds fill with reasons to not go, something in us remains on the starting line. We hear, "On your mark, get set," and our uncertainty and fear reach a peak. We hear "Go!" and the race has started. We take a step forward, and the race before us doesn't seem as daunting; each step is a step closer to our goal.

Just starting for me looked like researching home-based businesses. Just starting can look like applying to the school you want to go to, asking your boss for what you want and need, going out and meeting people, waking up ten minutes earlier to spend time with God or meditate. Just starting means knowing your dream and taking the first step toward that dream becoming a reality.

YOU CAN DO HARD THINGS

REFLECTION:

List five things you think are keeping you from pursuing your dream. You are at the starting line, what is keeping you from starting the race? Maybe you feel like it's not the right time to start pursuing your dreams? Maybe you feel comfortable with your life as it is now, maybe you have settled in your discomfort. Take some time to reflect on what is holding you back from taking the first step.

List five practical ways you can make time for your dreams, even if it's just ten minutes every day. Start practicing those this week. Even small steps lead to big change.

Chapter 2

YOU CAN FIND YOUR WHY

> **THE EXCUSE:**
> I don't have a good reason to dream.

I'm unmotivated and discouraged by my circumstances, and I just don't feel like dreaming right now.

I used to be a dancer. I started dancing when I was three years old, and it quickly became a passion of mine. It was more than a hobby or interest; my dance company also became a community that I could lean on, a group of people who supported me and helped me accomplish more than I could on my own, especially during those awkward adolescent years.

When my first daughter was born, my mind filled with dreams that I had for her. I wanted her to feel loved, supported, confident, and self-assured. I wanted her to be able to accomplish whatever she set her mind to. I wanted to be able to provide every opportunity for her, just as my parents had provided so many opportunities for me. And because dance held such a special place in my heart, I wanted to share that with my daughter. I wanted to give her the chance to experience the same joy and growth that I experienced through dance.

When my daughter was three years old, I decided it was time to enroll her in her first dance class! I was definitely much more excited than she was (and she was pretty darn excited). But when I looked up the price of the class and compared it with our monthly budget, it just didn't seem like we could make it work. I called John. I remember this day as if it was yesterday. I was pulling into the driveway of our home, and I asked John if I could enroll our almost three-year-old Josselyn into a ballet class for eighty dollars a month.

John paused and then said to me over the phone, "Babe, how are we going to pay for that?"

We had been using a budgeting system for a while that financial advisor Dave Ramsey recommended. Give each budget category an envelope, put your budgeted amount of cash in the envelope, and that's all there is for the month. As a young married couple, we were trying so hard to stay afloat financially, and this system had often been a lifesaver. As I started flipping through my mental file of our envelopes, a pit started forming in my stomach. I heard the pause in John's voice too.

John then said to me over the telephone, "What envelope is that going to come from?"

We had a grocery envelope and a mortgage envelope and a bills envelope. But no ballet envelope. My heart sank. We literally had nowhere to pull that extra eighty dollars from.

Here's the difference between me and my husband, and maybe you can relate. John is the ever smart, good, and trustworthy financial planner. And me? Well, let's just say if I had twenty bucks, it would burn a hole in my pocket until I spent it! John, on the other hand, would want to save this twenty-dollar bill until he was 120 years old. He would then proceed to take it to his grave and probably earn interest on it from six feet under. We are total opposites. But as frugal and wise as John is, he has always wanted to give me the world. He always tried to say yes to me when we could swing it.

To my dismay, at that moment in our life when I called John, we didn't have even the extra money for a dance class. It was just eighty dollars a month—but we didn't have any extra cash to spare. This was a huge wake up call to me. I knew that money was tight, but it wasn't until now that I realized my dreams for my children were having to shrink to fit our budget.

I was devastated. When I imagined my life and my girls' lives, this was not part of the picture. I closed my eyes and envisioned our children's lives. I saw them in dance class, playing sports, taking music lessons, doing all the extracurricular activities that they wanted to do. I saw a life of family vacations, which we had not yet been able to do with our kids. I saw a life of no financial struggle. But here I was in my driveway with no envelope for my family's dreams.

Thinking back to my own childhood, I remember my parents arguing about finances at times. Usually, it was because my mom wanted to do anything and everything possible for my siblings and me, and my dad, on the other hand, was trying to be realistic. He was looking at what was being deposited into the bank account versus what was being spent. My mom wanted to give us the world, but the finances weren't always there. I began to see the same exact story playing out for John and me.

For the first time since having my girls, I paused and actually dreamed of what I wanted for my kids. That day in my car changed my life; it changed my children's lives. I decided enough was enough. My kids and family were worth more. I refused to settle, and instead, I was going to dream again. I finally found my "why."

> **THE TRUTH:**
> We have to understand the "why" behind our dreams in order to work toward achieving them.

Whys help us identify our motivation and give us a reason to keep working toward our dream.

So many of us have made the excuse that we lack motivation when it comes to our dreams. We think we have to be ready to go on some big existential journey, and we just don't have the energy. And it's not our fault that we default to being overwhelmed by the mere idea of dreaming. We hear an awful lot about finding our purpose in life. Doesn't it seem like everyone's always talking about purpose? I think that language can be a little intimidating. Purpose sounds so big and meaningful and official. To me, asking "What is your purpose?" is a little scarier than simply asking "Why should I pursue this?" Searching for a "why" can be as simple as: *I want to have enough extra income for my daughters to take a dance class.*

When we approach our dreams from this direction, I really believe we can start to gain some traction and hone in our motivations. I don't think I will ever fully know my grand purpose in all my days on earth, but I should be able to know why I want to work towards a dream. The truth is that understanding your "why" is crucial. When it comes to dreaming, having a "why" at the foundation of your dream is really important for a few reasons.

1. Whys Are Motivating

That very same day I realized we couldn't afford dance, I joined a direct sales business as a way of making extra money for my family. My why started out as wanting to meet a financial need. I wanted to send my daughter to an eighty-dollars-a-month dance class. And because I could finally name that reason for going after a dream, I had a real-life motivation that pushed me to jump over that starting line we talked about in the first chapter. As scary as it felt to dream in our tight financial circumstances, I knew it was time to make a move, and I knew why I was doing it.

I will share more in later chapters about the vision exercises I started implementing to grow my business, but for now, what I want to reiterate is I suddenly possessed the motivation to go after my dreams. Knowing that I had a very concrete reason to work hard made me work harder.

Maybe your first step in finding your why is actually trying to nail down what it is that will motivate you. I was able to quickly identify that working for more money in our envelopes to make my daughter's dance dreams possible was why enough. But it might not be so straightforward for you. In order to get a hold of your motivation, stop and look around for some area of need or desire in your life that you want to answer. And it could be really simple. Why take on extra shifts at work? Because you want to buy new furniture to live in a home you love. Why stick to your meal plan? Because you want to be healthy and strong for your grandkids. Why start that blog? Because you love to be creative, and writing is your creative outlet. Instead of being burdened by our dreams, let our reasons why be what tell us to keep dreaming.

> **Instead of being burdened by our dreams, let our reasons why be what tell us to keep dreaming.**

FIND YOUR WHY

2. Whys Don't Rely Solely on Your Feelings

There are times in life when our feelings work in our favor. We are motivated, energized, excited, in love, focused—you name it. Those are the days when dreaming is fun and work is amazing and everything is awesome. I love those days. But then . . . then come the days when the feelings run out. When the work to achieve the dream no longer sounds appealing, when the kids were up all night crying, when you would rather lay on your couch and watch TV and drink a cup of coffee than go on that walk you said you'd go on. Feelings are powerful. They can completely control us and overrule our brains if we are not careful.

So what do feelings have to do with our dreams, and why is it important to have a why? When you think about that dream in your heart, it cannot just be a feeling. You cannot only work toward the dream when you feel like it. *But I'm a feeler, I'm a four on the Enneagram, I am emotionally driven*, you'll say. I get it, I really do have big feelings too! But feelings alone can't sustain your dream in the long run.

If I approached my marriage like so many people often approach working toward their dreams, we would be in trouble. If I only decided to be married when I felt like it, that would just really not work well for my husband. Or let's think for a second about our friendships. If girls only stayed friends with me when I was sweet, I would have no friends. Women of the world, hear me: your feelings change constantly. I'm sure you are fully aware of this. We learn in our adolescent years the joys of hormones and

YOU CAN DO HARD THINGS

roller-coaster emotions.

I'm well aware of this tension we have to navigate when it comes to dreaming. Some days, I feel like settling into my office and being laser focused. Kicking butt, taking names. I. am. Superwoman. Other days, I feel like drinking a latte while curled up on my couch, binge watching Hallmark Christmas movies, even if it is not Christmas. This is a real thing we have to wrestle with! Over the past five years of actually going after my dreams for my family, I quickly learned the hard way that achieving your dreams is not based on feelings. You can't just work toward your dreams on days where you "feel like it." We cannot work based on how we feel! Because, you guessed it, our feelings are constantly changing.

If you are married, take a moment and think about your sweet husband. Do you show up for your marriage on just the days you feel like it? Do you love your spouse only on the days he makes you happy and brings you breakfast in bed? I hope not. Because truly, if your husband is bringing you breakfast in bed every morning, we need to chat about where he was trained.

My husband does not bring me breakfast every day, but guess what? Even on the Tuesday mornings I'm making myself plain toast, I am committed to my marriage. I am not walking away. I'm there on the days my husband gives me butterflies and the smell of his cologne makes me want to play a little Marvin Gaye, but I also show up on the days he is on my last nerve and all I can smell is his bad breath, and if he tries to kiss me with his scratchy, unshaved whiskers one more time, I might punch him. Why do I stay and keep working at our relationship? Why? Because I am committed. Because I said 'til death do us part. I love him, even on the days I may not feel like I do. I want my children to grow up seeing what a godly marriage, not perfect marriage, looks like. And I want them to know that feelings are not the ultimate compass for their lives. I want to instill in them values of commitment and steadfastness.

And so, in the same way I show up for my marriage, I show up for my dreams—even when I don't always feel like it. Why do I do that? Because I know the whys behind my work on a very deep level, and my why doesn't change with my mood. I wanted to build a business so that my family could have a second stream of income. I wanted to relieve some of the financial stress from my husband. I wanted us to have some breathing room in our finances. At thirty-five, I have been able to surpass the income my parents, my grandparents, and my great grandparents made. Hear me when I say this: money is not everything, and every day I strive to live my life with eternity in mind, but I also want to live a life of freedom. I want freedom to give back when the Lord leads me to, freedom to travel where and when we want, freedom to send my children to the school I want them to go to. I want to live a life of freedom and abundance. This is why I get up every day and consistently work hard to achieve my goals.

Even if I don't want to work based on how I feel, I work based on what it is that I want. I work based on my why. Don't live your life, mother your children, love your spouse, work on your business, or pursue your dream based on how you feel. Rather, grab onto that why. Know what it is you want, and let that be what you fall back on, not your mood.

3. Your Why Can Grow

My why started with eighty dollars for ballet. That's why I was starting out in the direct sales business. Eighty bucks! And as I started to work for this why, I realized it started to grow. I found myself thinking, *Maybe I could make enough income to have Starbucks money, maybe even some Target money.* Then I thought, *What if I could pay for a family vacation to Disneyland!* It then grew to, *What if I could teach others how to do what I am doing?* I had to set these little goals along the way, but they were *why* I was waking up early and staying up late.

My why grew, and now one of my biggest whys is to change the future for my children and their children. I am changing the trajectory of my family. And I want to inspire others to do the same.

For far too long, women have believed the lie that they can't dream, they missed their chance, they are too old, they aren't smart enough, special enough, they don't have what it takes, someone else is already doing what they should have done, etc. That is anything but the truth. No matter how big or small your why is or how idealistic or silly your why may seem to you, your why matters. Whatever dream and whatever why you have is valid and

FIND YOUR WHY

important. Begin there with that one little thing that will edge you over the starting line. Then open yourself up to the possibilities of what can happen and grow when you're motivated and not just working on your feelings. Trust me, your why will start to grow too.

***

What is your dream and what is your why? What is it that will get you up a little earlier and cause you to stay up a little later? If you do not have a why, then when the going gets tough, when you hit that brick wall, when things seem to be at a standstill or someone rejects you or you don't feel like working anymore, you will quit. There have been countless times I have wanted to stop, throw in the towel, and give up. But then I remember: I am building my business so my children will live a life of freedom and choices. I am building my business to show my kids that you can do anything and everything that you set your mind to. I am building a business so I can give back in extraordinary measures. You have dreams in your heart, but in order to make your dreams a reality, you have to know the why behind them. The why is what separates dreams from passive wishes.

> **Whatever dream and whatever why you have is valid and important.**

You have a responsibility to go after your dreams.

YOU CAN DO HARD THINGS

Those dreams were birthed in your heart for a reason. You have to care for, protect, and bring life to them, and that all begins with knowing your why. Some days you may feel like it and some days you won't, but do it anyway! We have to hold on tight to our whys and let them push us through the storms, through the valleys, through the lows. When you find your why, a strong why, the how will take care of itself, and you will be motivated to overcome any obstacle that comes your way. In order to keep yourself on track, start listing all the reasons big and small of why you want to achieve your dreams. And then read that list every day. Remind yourself why you are doing what you do. Don't just make wishes. Dream big and know your whys.

FIND YOUR WHY

REFLECTION:

What is the why behind your dream?

What are some feelings and thoughts that get in the way of you pursuing that dream?

Make a list of your big and small whys behind your dreams.

Chapter 3

YOU CAN FAIL FORWARD

> **THE EXCUSE:**
> If I really go after my dream, I'm going to fail.

I would rather not pursue my dreams and be safe from failure than be seen as a failure by others.

As I started to grow my business and see success, I started thinking, *I should share what I am learning. Maybe I will even write a book about it.* I needed to take some small steps toward this dream first, so one of my best friends sent me a link to a popular mom blog that was looking for writers willing to share their story.

My friend knew I had a dream to write a book, and let me tell you, she is one of the most encouraging girls on the planet. She believed in me and thought this blog submission would be a great opportunity for an aspiring writer. So I clicked on the link, I read over the information, and got to the part where they wanted you to submit a sample entry. They wanted to see how you wrote, what kind of content you could bring, and if you would be a good fit for their site.

It was right about then when I deleted the email and slammed my laptop shut. Thoughts of *"You can't write. You can't even spell. They would never like what you have to say,"* filled my head. I jumped so quickly from the possibility of being an author to negative self-talk and the terrifying reality that other people could read this. Like on the internet. I went on to think that even if the blog did want me to be one of the writers, what if the audience didn't like my content? What if my blog entries were the ones with practically no views? And then my work would sit in some dark corner of the internet, gathering dust and whispering to me, *"You're not a writer."* Lies, lies, lies. My mind was flooded with lies that stemmed from my insecurities.

So how does the story end? There is no story. I was too scared to take a chance. I opted out and didn't submit an entry. Sure, I protected my heart from possible rejection or failure, but now I will never know what could have been. What if one of my entries could have given encouragement to that one mom running a business? What if I had the exact words that one overwhelmed, struggling mama needed to hear? What if what I said could have caused that mom to decide to take a chance and go after her dream? I don't know. I chose what I thought to be the easier, less painful route. I chose the "failure free" option.

But I look back and wonder: did I really spare myself from failure? I think those feelings of regret and wondering what could have been may be just as equally painful as trying. I realized not trying was the true failure.

***

After the blog fear I felt, I still couldn't shake the idea that I had something to say. I really began to feel the Lord leading me to write this book, but I was scared of how massively I'd flop if I actually tried. But this time, I took one tiny step against fear and spent a summer writing a manuscript. After writing this manuscript, I had no idea what my next step was. So, I went to my trusty friend Google and searched "how to publish a book."

After hours of research, it seemed my next step was to find a publisher. I started Googling publishing companies and found out the majority of publishers do not take unsolicited manuscripts. If you are like I was a few months ago and have no clue what that means, basically it means that most publishers will only look at manuscripts brought to them by a literary agent. (You mean to tell me I can't just send in this Word document and get it printed by Penguin Random House!)

I kept digging in my research and started talking with a friend familiar with the process. That friend told me that typically, literary agents want to see a query letter or proposal first, not your full manuscript. So then, I got to work and made a proposal. I was ready to send my proposal to some agents. After doing some more research (thank you again, Google), I found the contact information for a literary agent who represents one of my very favorite authors. I held my

YOU CAN DO HARD THINGS

breath in hopes that this could be my big break, and I hit send. Not long after I sent in the proposal, I received a reply that said, while my project sounds interesting, it is not right for her list at this time.

Ugh. Rejection. Now came that flood of negative thoughts that fed my insecurities and fears. Had I just wasted a whole summer writing a book when I could have spent that time with my kids? Was my book idea complete nonsense? Had too many people already written the same thing I was writing? I could have stopped, thrown in the towel, powered down the laptop, and called it quits. My greatest fear of being rejected and failing seemed to be coming true.

But I didn't want to live with that pain of giving up on a dream. And graciously, the Lord brought the right person into my life who told me about another literary agent who, in all honesty, sounded like a much better fit for me! She was the agent of the very book I was currently listening to on audio. So once again, I sent in my book proposal. A few days passed and I received a response that she loved my proposal and wanted to get to know me better. My first round of failure was not the finish line. You see, failure is inevitable. If you aren't failing, I would venture to say you aren't trying. It is not falling down, or being rejected, or making a mistake that matters;

> **It is not falling down, or being rejected, or making a mistake that matters; it is what you decide to do after that counts.**

FAIL FORWARD

it is what you decide to do after that counts.

***

When we look at human history, there are countless examples of failures—some big and some small. And for just as many times as we have failed, we can find those stories of individuals who demonstrated grit and resilience. More than just me and my initial failure to blog, plenty of other women in history have fallen harder and still gone on to reach higher. As I have thought more about dreaming, I have loved taking a look at others who failed, were told no, and experienced setbacks but did not let that stop them from chasing their dreams.

Joanne dreamed of being a writer. She spent years writing her stories while working full-time. Even when her dream seemed far-fetched and she was rejected by many publishers, she refused to give up. When she finally found a publisher, she was asked to not use her name because boy readers may not want to read a book about a boy wizard written by a female. As a result, she published under the name J.K. Rowling. Her Harry Potter series is the best-selling book series in history![1]

Oprah, one of the most influential women of my lifetime, started out as an evening news anchor in Baltimore. But a few months into the job, she was told by a Baltimore TV producer that she was "unfit for television news." Oprah was fired from her evening news reporter gig because she got too emotionally invested

YOU CAN DO HARD THINGS

in her stories. She then landed a role on a daytime TV show, which became a huge hit and lead to the launch of *The Oprah Winfrey Show*.[2]

Anna Wintour was fired from her first job as a junior editor after nine months at *Harper's Bazaar*. In 1988, she was named editor and chief of *Vogue*. She is, without a doubt, one of the most successful women in the fashion industry.[3]

Julia Child was fired as an advertising manager in the early 1930's from a home furnishing company. She didn't let one set back make her feel like a failure. She later went on to pursue her passion for French cooking, attend Le Cordon Bleu cooking school, write her acclaimed cookbook *Mastering the Art of French Cooking*, and become a television icon with her cooking shows.[4]

When I look at these women who have lived through failure and still kept going after a dream, I am inspired all over again to not let "no" be the final word. Oftentimes, our setbacks become our greatest setups. Sometimes it takes being told no to ignite that fire that propels you to go forward and fight for that yes! Conversely, I can't help but think of the other names, the names we will never know because instead of getting back up when they failed or were rejected, they stayed down. They threw in the towel; they quit. I don't know about you, but I don't want to be one of those women who stayed knocked down. We must

> **Oftentimes, our setbacks become our greatest setups.**

FAIL FORWARD

start to shift our perspective from thinking of any failure or rejection as a step backwards, and instead reorient ourselves to think of failures as still moving us forward toward our dream.

This is harder said than done. Maybe you failed at a dream, but instead of trying again you have straight up quit. You threw in the towel, and you are done. Maybe your failure came at the mercy of someone else, like losing your job or having to clean up someone else's mess they left behind. Whatever it is, I will admit, that feeling of utter let down when you fail is the worst. Any time I have failed at something, it is almost like pieces of my confidence were chiseled away. Because failure can be that deeply personal.

There's a moment in the movie *You've Got Mail* that, to me, captures what it feels like when we fail. Tom Hanks plays Joe Fox, a big-shot bookstore owner, and Meg Ryan plays Kathleen Kelly, owner of a small bookstore that's going out of business because of her rival Mr. Fox himself.[5] Joe says to Kathleen when her shop has to shut down: "Well it's not personal, it's business." And she responds in a very heartfelt manner: "What's that supposed to mean? I am so sick of that. All that it means was that it wasn't personal to you. But it was personal to me. It's personal to a lot of people. And what's so wrong with being personal anyways."

When we put our heart into our dreams, we are the only ones who know just how personal the failure can feel. There is a depth of the hurt or sense of regret we internalize because no, it wasn't just business. It

YOU CAN DO HARD THINGS

was personal when I failed. But this is part of learning to dream anyway. This is a key part of learning to fail forward. To go after these dreams, we recognize that it's probably going to hurt when we trip up or fall flat on our face. We can actually find some bit of hope or maybe even confidence knowing that, yes, it's going to sting when I fail because it is so personal. Because my dream means that much to me. And yet, we dream anyway. We take a step in faith and prepare for the failure.

It changed my life when I heard a speaker say you sometimes have to fail forward. Yes—fail forward! So, you didn't get that job, you missed your deadline, you didn't get that promotion, you got out of your workout routine, or you blew your diet. That stinks, it really does. And I know as well as any, it is really easy to internalize this sense of shame and failure and take it really personally. Because like Kathleen says, it is personal! But let's start adding these questions to the mix: Did you get a little closer to what you were going for? Did you learn something about yourself? Did you grow stronger? I bet you anything the answer is yes to at least one of those questions! I mean, you started, didn't you? You went for it for some amount of time. So, it's time to try again. Don't even think of going backwards. Just keep moving, even if it means failing forwards. There is no denying that it is so much easier to retreat than to get back up. But what does retreating do? It does nothing. You can quit, back down and live a life of "What Ifs", or you can decide to learn from your mistakes and be better the next time.

FAIL FORWARD

***

In order to change our perspective when it comes to failure, we must first take stock of why we are afraid of failing. What is at stake? Taking stock of your situation helps you to logistically plan and map out what achieving your dream will take, which builds confidence and belief in yourself. Because the fear of failure inhibits us from believing that we can make our dreams and goals a reality, we must change our mindset. There are a million quotes about failure, but I love this one from author Paulo Coehlo: "There is only one thing that makes a dream impossible to achieve: the fear of failure."[6] Failure is the one thing that will completely prevent us from even trying to make our dreams a reality. If we let our fear become more pronounced than our faith, we will never move forward in our lives. We will never achieve our dreams.

As we think about failure, it is also important to recognize who you are afraid of disappointing. Are you afraid of failure because you think people will look down on you? Or are you afraid that failing will validate your own insecurities? Understanding why we are so scared of failure is like our parents turning on the closet light to show us there's not a monster inside of it. When we can believe and see that everyone fails at something, we can have more faith in ourselves and our dreams—faith that is unaffected by "scary" circumstances.

Belief is crucial because it allows you to have faith in yourself that is unaffected by circumstances. When you know your identity, then you can weather any failure that comes your way. Believing in yourself also helps you navigate and stay afloat when others' opinions and rejection of you comes, because those things will come. But when you aren't fixated on fear and others' opinions of you, then you can focus on your dream.

> **THE TRUTH:**
> **We can't let fear of failure stand in our way.**

Even if we fail, we will fail forward and will learn through the process.

I think a "failure" or a "mistake" should simply be called a lesson learned or a learning experience. But you know why it can't be called that? Because not everyone will take their failures and their mistakes and learn from them.

I will admit, this fear of failure has held me back countless times in my life. Not even failure itself, just the idea of it. And as a result, I tell myself: *If I don't start, I can't fail.* And sometimes I think: *Maybe if I kind of start but just give it 20 percent of my effort, then if I fail, it won't hurt quite as bad.* It is hard to take risks, try something new, attempt the unknown. We should be encouraged when we remember 2 Timothy 1:7, "For God has not given us a spirit of fear, but of power and of love and of a sound mind" (NKJV), and Romans 8:31, "If God is for us, who can be against us?" (MEV). What are we scared of? Once, I was too scared to pursue my dream of writing. I nearly quit on the dream of writing this book because my proposal got rejected. Really, I did. I almost said, "Nope, there's no way this girl could type up anything worth your time." But I didn't let that no have the last word.

Have you ever heard it said that our greatest battle is the six inches between our ears? We have a battlefield of our minds that we face every single moment of every day. In her bestselling book *Battlefield of the Mind*, Joyce Meyer says, "When a person is going through a hard time, his mind wants to give up. Satan knows that if he can defeat us in our mind, he can defeat us in our experience. That's why it is so important that we not lose heart, grow weary and faint."[7] In my business, I have people who join my team every month, and I can almost always tell immediately when someone joins my team how successful they will be. Those that come in with belief and confidence that they are going to rock it usually do! And those people who aren't confident . . . their actions typically follow their belief. If you believe you can, you can. If you believe you can't, you can't. End of story. The good news is you can change your belief at any time. So, if you lack belief, you are not doomed forever. You are just momentarily doomed. The key to stop doubting yourself

> **When you know your identity, then you can weather any failure that comes your way.**

and quit fearing failure is to "take captive every thought" (2 Corinthians 10:5). Stop letting negative thoughts and fears fill your mind; take them captive. Press pause, and meet the negative thought with truth.

Philippians 4:13 is my favorite verse, and I believe it's God's great encouragement to us when we start to feel like our risk of failure is too great: "I can do all things through Christ who gives me strength" (BSB). All things! When is the last time you actually believed this?

If your mind starts wandering to thoughts of "I could never start my own business; I'm not smart enough," try taking that thought captive and replacing it with "I can start my business because Christ gives me strength." What about when you start saying, "I am not qualified to be in the job I'm in. They should've given it to someone else . . . " Nope! "I am qualified to do this job because Christ gives me strength." I am not perfect, I am not immune to failing, but in my weakness, God is strong and He gives me what I need to be the mom, wife, business owner, and friend He needs me to be. Take your fear-filled thoughts captive and encourage yourself by speaking your unshakable identity in Christ over yourself.

I heard a story once about a person going in for a job interview. This person answered the questions the interviewer asked, and at the end, the interviewer said, "Do you have questions for me?" The job applicant replied, "What would you do if you knew you could not fail?" And the interviewer started crying, right there in the conference room, because she realized she was scared to

FAIL FORWARD

do what she actually dreamed of doing. Maybe this is one of those motivational stories people share on LinkedIn, but it strikes a chord of what we've been talking about this whole chapter. We are told to shrink our dreams for fear of failure, and yet, we are still left with that pain that lingers when we don't go after our dreams.

So know that yes, your dreams might scare you. But as you take these fears captive, take heart and learn that if you're going to fail, at least you're failing forward.

YOU CAN DO HARD THINGS

REFLECTION:

What are you most scared of failing at?

What would you do if you knew you would not fail?

What are some lies you believe that keep you from pursuing your dreams? Cross out those lies and write down the truths according to the Word of God.

What are some ways you can replace those lies with unshakable truths?

Chapter 4

YOU CAN HAVE VISION

> **THE EXCUSE:**
> My dreams are impossible.

Of course there are things that would be amazing to be or do, but those are just impossible and not real life. I shouldn't even fantasize about my dream becoming a reality because it will just get my hopes up for something that can't actually happen.

When I think about vision and belief, I think about the four-minute mile. On May 6, 1954, Roger Bannister was the first man to finally beat the four-minute mile.[8] For years, experts said that no human could physically run a mile in less than four minutes. They believed it to be physically impossible. In the 1940s, the mile record was 4:01, where it stood for nine years. Why did no other runner beat that record? I can almost bet anything it is because they were told they couldn't, and therefore, they believed they couldn't. I don't think there was anything physically holding these athletes back. Rather, they were held back by a psychological barrier. Why would anyone see themselves beating a record they were told was impossible to break? As I studied this story, what stood out to me was Roger Bannister's vision. While training, Roger consistently visualized himself breaking the record in order to create a sense of certainty on his body and mind. Sure enough, he broke the record with a 3:59.4 mile. He saw it, trained for it, and then achieved it. What is really mind-blowing is that once he showed the world this record could be broken, another runner did it, and another, and another. Now, there are even high school athletes who can run a sub-four-minute mile.

What is your four-minute mile? What is that thing, that dream, that goal that you are too scared to visualize? Like those other runners in the 1950s, we create these psychological barriers to our dreams. Why exert energy on something that is impossible? Why waste my time if I don't think my dream is achievable? These are the kind of questions we plant in our hearts, and as a result, we are shutting off our vision for what might be. We have to teach ourselves to train with a sense of certainty, cultivating vision for impossible things. Instead of dooming your dream as a failure from the start, I want you to see yourself doing it, crushing it, running that three-minute and

> **We have to teach ourselves to train with a sense of certainty, cultivating vision for impossible things.**

HAVE VISION

fifty-nine-second mile.

Even before I heard the story of Roger Bannister, I was a huge believer in visualizing what it is that you want. In my own life, I pictured so many of my greatest accomplishments in my head long before they ever happened. But I can just as easily think back on things I wanted but didn't achieve because I let doubt keep me from ever even envisioning my goal. Usually, the moment my mind would start to think about "What if?" and begin to dream, doubt, insecurity, and fear dressed up as the "voice of reason" would hold me back from dreaming. I truly believe if you can let go of the fear of failure, the fear of what others may think, and all the fearful "What Ifs"... you can become limitless. This freedom to pursue what others would say is impossible is only within reach if you can allow yourself to dream and not let insecurity cloud your vision.

I recently was chatting with a friend and she said, "You are really good at selling a dream." I wasn't quite sure how to take that statement, so I pondered this for days after. Sure, with my health and wellness company, I sell products as well as a business opportunity. But I don't sell a pre-packaged dream. As I've continued to think on what my friend said, I know I am a dreamer who is passionate about helping others believe in themselves. But I'm not just trying to sell people an opportunity to join my team; I want to sell people on the whole idea of dreaming. Because yes, I am one of those crazy people who truly believes that your dreams can come true. I also believe

YOU CAN DO HARD THINGS

that being around a dreamer makes dreaming contagious! Doctors are coming up with cures and treatments for cancer, authors are becoming New York Times bestsellers, aspiring actors and actresses are landing roles in hit TV shows and Academy Award-winning films. Are they lucky? I don't know, maybe. But I can guarantee you one thing: they have vision, they aren't scared to dream, and they are actively going for it. Do you want to be the person that says, "It can never happen for me, so I am not going to even try," or do you want to be one of the ones crazy enough to dream it up and go after it? And honestly, dreaming isn't crazy. Someone is going to do it, so why not you? Why not me? Why can't we have big vision and dream? Remember what I have said: even in the worst-case scenario, we fail forward and dust ourselves off to try again.

***

Before we dive into the nitty gritty of what it looks like to implement vision and belief, we need to talk about why it's important. We hear this phrase a lot, "What you sow, you will reap." So, let's take some time to think about what that means for our own dreams. We become what we believe, period. You can make a choice to plant seeds of belief, or you can plant seeds of unbelief. You can plant seeds of vision, or you can decide to not plant anything new. But, either way, what you plant will start to grow.

A few months ago, I got on this kick where I was

reading about every break-in, burglary, kidnapping, etc. I was obsessed and fixated on all these instances of invasion. Now, I will stand by the notion that it is good to be informed and it is wise to make sure you lock your door and set your alarm if you have one. But what is not good is to be consumed with fear. I was becoming fearful and freaking out if my husband forgot to lock a door or left the garage door open. Before I knew it, my youngest daughter Julianna had picked up on my fear, and she was worried about burglars and being kidnapped. She was coming in our room crying at night. We were having to check under her bed and in her closet to show her that everything was okay. I quickly realized I had been sowing fear into my kids.

I can see this same principal in my business as well. When I am leading from the front, when I am excited, when I am casting vision, my team follows suit. When I am dreaming loudly and encouraging others, they want to do that too. The seeds you scatter affect your own garden as well as those that are in close proximity to you. Take a moment and ask yourself: What is your sphere of influence? Where is it that you are planted? What are you sowing and how is it impacting those around you?

Just as what we sow affects our families and our businesses, the same is true with our personal dreams. When I believe I can achieve the goals I set, when I have a good mindset and am thinking positive, I become unstoppable. I start accomplishing my goals! But if I let the doubt that can often times creep in takeover, you better believe my garden starts to grow and sprout those seeds and weeds of doubt. I shut the laptop instead of writing the book on my heart. I scale back the business goal I set at the beginning of the month. I talk myself out of pursuing that hobby I so badly wanted to begin.

When I think about farmers and gardeners who plant seeds, I think about how many of those seeds are planted with hope of harvest. Each year, every seed is planted in expectation that new things will grow from them, even though farmers know farming will be difficult at times. They know not all seeds yield a big crop. That sometimes, there's bad weather or no rain. But nevertheless, seeds are sown with vision for harvest time.

This idea of reaping what I sow finally took root in my heart, and suddenly, all it took was one day of me deciding to just close my eyes and visualize a better life for my family. I made the choice to plant seeds of vision and believe that things could be different. That I could dream and see things in life change. Why can't my girls go to dance class? Why can't we have more money each month? Why can't we live a life of abundance and be able to give back? So, I say to you today: Why not you? What are you planting? What harvest are you envisioning?

***

Belief and vision are not just things that you are born with. You can grow them; you can acquire more of them. Belief and vision are muscles that you have to work out

HAVE VISION

daily. Our main problem we run up against is we often forget how to cultivate these basic practices. We don't believe in ourselves or can't let ourselves see any new realities. We make excuses. We are afraid. We think our dreams are nuts! Over the last few years, I've been training myself to sow belief and vision, and I have reaped greater rewards than when I sowed self-doubt and fear. How can we start to chip away at our excuse of thinking our dreams are too crazy to come to life, and start claiming the truth that our dreams *are* possible?

> **Belief and vision are muscles that you have to work out daily.**

When I started my business in direct sales five years ago, I had no clue what I was doing. Despite my lack of knowledge, I made the choice to envision myself being successful! I saw myself promoted to each rank and even pictured myself earning a crazy $10,000 bonus the company advertised. I then took it a step further and saw myself going to the next rank and the next rank, and eventually, I saw myself at the very highest rank of the company. I mean, why not, right? I would see myself as a top income earner. I dreamed of making one million dollars in commissions! I envisioned my team growing to hundreds then to thousands. Sure, I had maybe 500 Facebooks friends and 200 Instagram followers, but why couldn't I one day lead a team of thousands if I worked hard enough? I even saw myself speaking on the stage at

YOU CAN DO HARD THINGS

the company conferences in packed arenas.

A few months after joining, I went to my company's annual conference. I sat in the back of a massive arena filled with 10,000 people. I am blind as a bat, and I had to squint to see the stage and the speakers. They looked more like little ants than people, and I hated being so far back. The whole time I sat there, I told myself that next year I would not only be sitting in the front of that arena where the top-level VIP distributors sat, but I would be on that stage. I even saw myself getting to know the founders and CEOs of the company and becoming friends with them. Having vision motivated me to work harder at my job. Rather than just embracing mediocrity, I told myself all those dreams were possible. I unashamedly envisioned all those dreams coming true. You guys, I am not kidding when I say vision matters. I truly believe that when you begin something, it is crucial to stop and visualize what you want to happen!

Now, I am not saying that everything you dream up will happen, but on the flip side, why can't it? I bet you every president of the United States first saw themselves as a president! They probably pictured themselves sitting in that glorious Oval Office countless times before they were actually elected. And I bet you every movie star saw herself on the big screen, at red carpet premiers, signing autographs, being cast in movies with other celebrities way before it actually happened. And I bet every New York Times bestselling author dreamed of the day her name and her book would be on that list years before she sat down to write.

HAVE VISION

Now you might be reading this thinking: *"I don't want to be president. Hollywood acting? No way. And writing a book would be pure torture."* And that's okay, because no two dreams are exactly alike. But my guess is, there's something that sparked your imagination and made your heart beat a little faster. What is it that you want? What is that one thing that you can't stop thinking about, that you desire so badly? Close your eyes. Yes, close your eyes right now and imagine it! See yourself. What does it look like? What does it smell like? What does it feel like? If you can see it, why can't you do it? Those of us who are crazy enough to see extraordinary things happen are the ones who actually make them happen.

Let me give you an analogy I once heard that really stuck with me. A ship doesn't leave harbor and set sail without a pre-planned destination. There is a map, a plan, and a compass that will lead it where it needs to go. It would be ridiculous for a ship to set sail into the ocean and just sail around. It would most likely wreck or get lost at sea. If that's true of an ocean voyage, shouldn't it be true of our lives too? Why do we live our lives aimlessly drifting without vision or a map of where we want to go?

Drifting is going through the motions of each day without having a goal set as to where you want to arrive. You might even say you have a dream, but if you are not actively pursuing it, you are drifting. Maybe you have a dream to get in shape and start a workout routine, but right now, your day is consumed with shuttling your kids to and from school and endless activities. You have not stopped to envision, think, or plan out how you can make this goal of yours a reality. And as a result, you go through life ignoring a dream you have in your heart. Maybe you work for a company but have this dream to start your own venture. Instead of visualizing exactly the kind of business you want and coming up with a strategic plan on how to start on your own, you settle with where things are safe and secure. I call that drifting. You are not living out your life to its fullest purpose.

As living, breathing human beings, we all have dreams and desires in our heart. Maybe you dream of being an intentional, present mom who is involved with her children's school and volunteers as part of the PTA. Maybe your desire is to start that online Etsy shop you always saw yourself running. For others, that dream may mean being promoted in your business or becoming partner. You have dreams specific to just you. But if you ignore them, stick them on the back burner, and tuck them away, I do not think you will ever be fully filled. Those dreams were birthed for a reason. So I want you to stop ignoring them, stop drifting and letting the days just pass you by, and stop for a moment and truly envision what it is you want to happen coming to pass.

***

Proverbs 29:18 says, "Where there is no vision, the people perish" (KJV), and I believe that to be deeply true. You have to have vision, or else you're like that drifting ship.

HAVE VISION

Vision for today, vision for this week, vision for this month, vision for this year.

Now that we understand the importance of vision, I want to share practical habits that I believe will help you cultivate vision for your life. First: write your dreams down on real paper. Recently, I read an article about goal setting by psychology professor Dr. Gail Matthews. Dr. Matthews conducted a study and found that you become 42 percent more likely to achieve your goals and dreams simply by writing them down on a regular basis.[9] So, last year, I started writing my dreams down daily—yes, daily. Every single morning, I wake up, do my devotion for the day, listen to some worship music, pray, and then I write down my ten dreams for the next ten years. Sure, I have those dreams memorized by now, but that doesn't matter. I still take that action step and put them onto paper in my journal daily. It is very powerful, and I challenge you to try it!

Each day that I write down my dreams, I start to feel a little more confident in accomplishing those dreams. Like I said, by now, this practice is second nature to me, but the first day I decided to do this, I was actually scared to write them down. I even thought about downsizing a few of the dreams in the beginning. Then I told my mind to shut it, and I just wrote them down anyway. Now I write them with a big, fat grin on face every morning at about 6:30 a.m. So get out a pen and piece of paper and starting writing out those beautiful, glorious, scary, intimidating dreams you see in your head.

YOU CAN DO HARD THINGS

Next, I want you to speak that dream out loud. Speak it out loud, shout it at the top of your lungs, say it in the shower. When I started my business back in 2014, I would pray in the shower. Maybe because my life was a bit crazy and my two girls were one and two years old, I didn't have a lot of personal quiet time. Normally there was a crying baby, a toddler repeatedly asking for a snack, and an episode of *Daniel Tiger's Neighborhood* playing in the background . . . at all times. So the shower was my solitude, even though I probably only got three of those a week. Every time I managed to make it in the shower, I would speak my goals and dreams out loud, as nutty as it sounds. "I am a top income earner." "I am a millionaire," "I have a successful business and an exploding team." "I am one of our church's top givers." I would get super specific with what I spoke. And guess what happened . . . those dreams came true. Not all of them, but a lot of them. And the ones that haven't come true yet, they will. It may take time. But I have envisioned them, I have written them down, and I am speaking them out as if they have happened.

You might be thinking it seems a bit absurd that I take time to write out a bunch of dreams that have not yet happened, and then say them out loud as if they have happened—daily. And I don't know, maybe it is a tad unusual. But something changes in me when a dream goes from being a mere wish I have in my heart to something I can actually visualize happening. When I write and speak my dream out loud, it starts to become real.

HAVE VISION

***

As I've taken hold of these habits and practices, I've now started seeing the fruit of them in my family as well. My claim to fame as a mother used to be that I scared my kids into having nightmares of kidnapping and home invasion. I am proud to say that now, they probably lie awake at night thinking about how they are going to achieve their huge dreams for their lives. What you sow, you will reap.

How did this happen? How did my girls go from being scared to being visionary? Every year for the past five years, my family has made vision boards together in January. This was something I learned to do when I began my own business. As soon as my girls were old enough to understand what it was I was doing every January, we started involving them. We sit down with poster boards, stickers, markers, magazines, glitter, and more glitter. We make a board of goals, wishes, desires, and accomplishments we want to see happen in the new year. I make one, John makes one, my girls Josselyn and Julianna each make one, and then we intentionally work the next twelve months on making those dreams become a reality.

Maybe you have never made a vision board. Let me tell you some of the things my family and I have whipped up for what has now become one of my favorite family traditions. Usually, my board has personal, family, marriage, health, business, and travel goals, as well as a word of the year to focus on. I like to think through each of these categories so that I'm not just thinking solely about my business as the only area of life where I am looking to grow and dream. I want the vision for my life and for my year to be holistic and well-rounded.

On my own board, one year I included a reading goal because I used to not be a reader. I mean, I guess I don't know if you would call me a reader now, because technically, I listen to audiobooks. But I'm counting this as a step up because I used to never listen or read anything except for my Bible. I thought I didn't have the time to read. This past year, I decided to stretch myself and put that I wanted to read one book a month for the whole year. Now, that may not sound like much to you, but to the girl who had probably read one book total in the last five years . . . it was a big deal. So, I wrote with my glitter pen that I wanted to read at least one book a month. And what happened? I ended up reading well over one book a month because it was something I was intentionally working on.

One year, I wrote "family dinners around the table" on my vision board. I had noticed that we started getting busy with life. I saw us begin to feed the girls, and John and I might eat later, or we would all eat on the bar stools at the island instead of sitting at the table. I realized I wanted to change things and get in the habit of us all sitting at the kitchen table and eating as a family every night. Years later, that is something we still implement because we intentionally set that as a goal.

I always put something on my dream board that has to do with my marriage. One year, I put weekly date

HAVE VISION

nights on there. What happened? John and I made it a priority to start having date nights. A couple years ago, we bought season tickets for the local theater so we would have a once-a-month date night there. Once again, it is about setting a goal, putting it on paper, and then making it a priority.

I usually have some sort of health goal on my board as well. This past year, I put that I wanted to get back to my pre-baby weight. My son, JJ, was only five months old when I made my board, and ten months later, I am proud to say I am back at my pre-baby weight. I have been eating healthy, taking my vitamins and supplements, and working all year to create healthy habits so that I could achieve this goal.

It is also important to me to set specific business goals on my board. I write monthly income goals, as well as what number income earner I want to be within my company since every year they put out those numbers. I also include goals for how much I want to have in my savings account as well as how much I want to give back above my tithe.

This past year, I put volunteering as a family on my board, and it was exciting to do that together with my girls over the holidays.

Vacations are one of my favorite things to put on my dream board. It gives me a goal to save and work towards. One year, I wrote down Lake Tahoe, which is where John and I got married. It was important for me to show my girls where we got married, so I put it on the board and we made sure to plan a trip there that year! I have passed on my love for traveling to my girls, so you better believe they put fun destinations on their boards as well. For two years, Josselyn put the Golden Gate Bridge on her board, so we made that dream come true for her with a fun trip to San Francisco. Julianna had Disney World on her dream board, and that was another fun trip we planned on their behalf. This past year, they both put the Eiffel Tower on their dream board, and lucky for them, Paris has always been a dream of mine. So guess where we are going this summer? Yup! Paris. One thing that's important to remember when it comes to vacationing is that the price tag doesn't equate to the quality of experience. I have a girlfriend who made her first dream board a couple years ago, and her focus was paying off debt. As a goal, she put a picture of her favorite hotel in her city on her dream board. That motivated her to work and save to intentionally plan a family weekend stay-cation. It is not always about the destination itself, but just making a fun memory together as a family.

My girls also put activities on their boards they want to do. I encourage my girls to think about school, hobbies, and experiences they want to reach for in the upcoming year. For instance, both of the girls put fishing on their boards. Don't ask me why because I am not an outdoorsy person, but they both wanted to go fishing. This year they both put camping on their boards, (I am not looking forward to that activity; I think I prefer glamping . . .) so

HAVE VISION

John is working on a father/daughter trip for them to take.

I always encourage my girls to set goals, whether those goals have to do with sports or school. They often add new things they want to try. Julianna is a gymnast and she has earning a medal on her board. She works hard in gymnastics and has been on pre-team this past year. In February, she moved up to Level 2 and has started competing. She has her heart and mind set on earning a medal, and I can't wait to watch her work towards pursing that goal.

One year, Josselyn wrote down that she wanted to "earn the Glow Award." Each week, the teachers at her school choose one child per grade that they notice shining brightly. These kids exhibit good behavior, they listen and respect their teachers, and help their peers when needed. I am not going to lie—this dream worried me a tad! I mean there are sixty-something kids with only thirty-something weeks in the school year, but Josse put it on her board. Let me tell you that there were a lot of happy tears in our home when our big girl earned the Glow Award that year. She worked hard, strived to be on her best behavior, and it was really neat to see that dream get checked off her board.

Every year, I pray for a word as well and put that on my board. It is a word I try to meditate on and think about throughout the year. The Lord has given me words like trust, intentional, and this year's word was expand.

I know these dream or vision boards might sound basic and simple, and the truth is, they are. But there is something about taking time to really visualize and see what you want for the upcoming year that makes you be extra intentional throughout the next twelve months. In my family, it amazes me to see those dreams that we first see come to fruition throughout the year. But it all begins with vision.

I want you to start writing out your dreams and declaring them as if they have already happened. This is not a one-time thing. I want you to do this every day—yes, every day. As time goes by, those things will change, those dreams will grow and your vision will expand and your belief in yourself will deepen. I don't know if you are going to visualize straight A's, graduating college, getting a new job, starting that new business, buying a home, paying off debt, but whatever it is, decide today to just SEE IT! I know it can be hard to dream, but remember you have to see it first. Take that first step of faith and visualize what you want for your future. Today, right now, decide to start having vision and belief for your life because you can, and know that you're not crazy for dreaming big.

> **THE TRUTH:**
> **Having vision and belief is never crazy.**

Vision is the only way that world-changing things are accomplished. Vision to see yourself actually accomplishing your dream can only lead to growth and prosperity. Don't sell yourself short.

HAVE VISION

I think back to myself at that first company conference, squinting on the back row as dreams of more took root in me. Do you want to know the craziest part of this story? ALL of those things I mentioned earlier in this chapter happened. Yes—every last one of them. Within twelve months, I had grown my team from five to thousands. I was a top income earner in the company, and I even spoke during one of the sessions on that exact stage one year later. I also had the incredible opportunity to get to know the CEOs of my company. And they were just as amazing as I had imagined. I believe with every fiber of my being that these things all came into existence because I first visualized them happening.

I remember living in our first teeny tiny apartment and visualizing one day owning a home with a huge living room where we could entertain, host Bible studies, and gather together with family and friends for holidays. Our living room now is literally the size of our first apartment, and the connection and ministry that takes place there is priceless to me.

I remember visualizing going to our CEOs' private island. In fact, I wrote it on one of my dream boards and guess what? I have had the honor of going to that amazing private island twice now.

I remember finally getting over my fear of writing a book and actually visualizing it happening, and here I am. But you better believe had I never visualized it, you wouldn't be reading this right now.

If you take a moment to think back on your goals,

accomplishments, and big wins in life so far, I can bet you almost anything they all started with that first thought. You had the courage to see it, to dream it. You might have not believed it yet, but you saw it and that is all that matters at the beginning.

As last year came to an end, I spent some time looking back at my dream board from the year. Once again, I am amazed at so many dreams I got to check off. We went on a family beach trip last spring, I reached my goal weight, I promoted in my business to the rank I wrote on my board, I exceeded the number of books I wanted to read each month, we have more in our savings account than the goal I wrote on my board, I was just announced the number two income earner in my company like I wrote, my business exceeded the number I had written for monthly sales, John and I have continued having monthly date nights, and we are going to be volunteering with our girls. Are there things that haven't happened . . . sure there are. But that's okay! They are going right back on my board for this year, because it is not a matter of if they will happen but simply when.

After my reflection on last year, I couldn't wait to work on my next board! We had a dream board party at our house with some friends and family this year. Among the things on my vision board: starting my second book and maybe even a devotional. I have recently partnered with an amazing organization that has a safe house for girls in Dallas escaping sex trafficking, so I have some big dreams regarding what I want to do for them. We have

HAVE VISION

some business goals as a family, and I already began to see little pieces of them coming to fruition last year. I know even more things will fall into place this year. I also have a number the Lord gave me, and I cannot wait to be able to write a check to our church for that amount; I am believing this will be the year.

YOU CAN DO HARD THINGS

REFLECTION:

Make a vision board. Use whatever material you want; make it unique to you. If you have never made a dream board, think of a goal you have for yourself in the following areas: personal, marriage, family, faith, travel, business, finances, and a word for the year to focus on. These dream boards hang somewhere we will see them daily. I have had them in my bedroom or my office. This year, I have mine in my closet where I look at it every day as I get dressed in the morning. You want to see this board every single day so you are reminded of these big, bold, audacious dreams you have.

List five dreams you want to accomplish and write them as if they have already happened (Example: I am president of my own company. I've written a book. I've graduated with a master's degree.) Be as specific as you can be!

Chapter 5

YOU CAN WORK FOR IT

> **THE EXCUSE:**
> I am comfortable where I am at.

Things are good right now. I mean, not everything is perfect, but things are manageable and that's really all I can ask for, right? In a perfect world, I'd make some changes, but change is hard and disruptive and just doesn't seem worth the effort. Working to actively achieve something doesn't seem necessary when things in my life are fine.

When I was growing up, I was diagnosed with some major learning disabilities. I couldn't read well. In fact, I couldn't read until my second time through third grade at almost ten years old. My brother was two years younger than me and clearly smarter than me. He started reading books when he was six, and I would look at the pages full of letters and not recognize a single word. School was hard. I knew I was in the slower reading group; I always had to go to tutoring and summer school. Even with all of that, I still struggled. I cheated in junior high and in high school. I was "hyperactive." My name was always on the board, so I was one of the kids who always had to sit on the curb and miss out on some or all of recess. I think most of my behavioral problems—not listening, always talking, getting in trouble—were a result of me trying to take attention off of my learning disabilities. Plus, when you don't understand what is being taught, why not chit-chat with your table partner next to you?

A few years after I graduated high school, I went to college to get my bachelor's degree. I wasn't quite sure if I could do it academically, but I wanted to try. I'll never forget that very first week of my freshman year in college. My biology professor put up a PowerPoint slide with adjectives of what an A student was like: driven, ambitious, goal-oriented, and hardworking. He then did the same for a B student, as well as a C, D, and even F student. As I sat there and read the adjectives describing each student on that PowerPoint, I said to myself: I want to be an A student! I *have* to be an A student. I then closed my eyes and saw myself graduating college with not just one A on my transcript but straight A's and a 4.0 GPA. I sat there in that little muggy college classroom in West Texas and dreamed up my next four years of college. I didn't know how someone who was diagnosed with learning disabilities—who even qualified for extra time on her SAT and other tests—was going to graduate with a 4.0 and get all A's, but baby, you bet I had the vision, and I was willing and ready to put in the necessary work!

WORK FOR IT

I decided to meet with each of my professors at the beginning of the semester and ask for the dates for all of the exams for that semester. At each meeting, I explained that I could not study for an exam just one week before like most students. It took me an entire month of studying every single day to be able to ace a test. I had to bring a tape recorder to class to record all of the lectures because I couldn't retain information in class. So, I would record it to play back over and over once I got back to my apartment. I would then make flash cards for every single exam and quiz myself. John and I got married while we were still in college. He would watch all the ways I had to study and tell me that I spent longer studying and preparing for one exam than he did for the entire semester, and that was 100 percent true. The thing is, John is gifted academically, and he doesn't have to put in nearly as much work to get an A. But that doesn't mean I can't get the same A that he can get. I will have to work harder and study more, but I, too, can get that A.

I most definitely could have still gone to college and graduated without a 4.0, because someone who gets all C's does, in fact, get the same diploma as someone who gets straight A's. But I had a dream, a burning desire, a goal to do something I had never done. I wanted to prove to myself I could do it. I, SheriLynn, could get straight A's. Four years and millions of flashcards later, I proudly walked across the stage graduating from The University of Texas of the Permian Basin with a 4.0, Magna Cum Laude. And boy . . . did I work for it. I'll be honest with you: I'm still a little bit amazed at myself when I think back on how I was able to graduate college with a 4.0 despite the things that could have held me back.

For so much of my childhood and teenage years, I made excuses for myself. While I didn't love the fact that I couldn't read well and school was difficult, I slid into a place of comfort with distraction and allowed myself to be content with academic difficulty. Learning the necessary skills and study habits to succeed would have been so much harder, and until I could envision more for myself, I really believed this was just the hand I was dealt. I believed I wasn't capable of doing hard things.

Getting that degree was one of the major milestones of my life, and tuning into that drive and determination was crucial for the rest of my story. I would have never been satisfied barely getting through college when I had a dream of proving to myself I could accomplish what seemed impossible. So when the opportunity came to join a company with opportunity for growth, I applied those same principles I applied to college. I could've done the bare minimum and earned that little bit of extra money for my daughter's dance class, but I was done being comfortable with my difficulties and knew that I was capable of working hard. Instead of my first question being "Why do I need to work any more than that?", my mindset was "What if I committed to more than that?"

Those little practices of envisioning great things for my future actually set me up to do the hard work. And now, when I think of how I started a business while being a stay-at-home mom with a one-year-old and a two-year-old and still went to the highest rank in the company in a year and a half, I am reminded that I can do hard things. I decided I was going to do these things, and once I made those choices, there was no stopping me. I may not be a magical unicorn, but I am a hard worker.

Because I struggled with learning disabilities, I have developed a work ethic that is unmatched. I would not be who I am today had I not lived through those struggles. If school had come easy, I do not know if I would have developed the determination to graduate college with a 4.0. Who knows if I would have had the drive to work my way to the top of a company in less than two years? I truly believe that a huge reason I am the way I am is because I had to learn how to compensate for my shortcomings. Yes, I wish I could read an actual paper book and comprehend what I was reading. I wish I could listen to a lecture and be able to understand and retain what the speaker said. But my struggles taught me how to rise up and persevere. I went from being a stay-at-home mom who felt not very smart most of her life to a business owner with a multimillion-dollar organization, leading a team of over 10,000 people. I still battle feeling inadequate, and it is uncomfortable to admit my struggles. Still, I embrace every lesson I learned during the difficult times because they helped shape me into the person I am today.

What is that obstacle you've become used to? That thing in your path that you've just accepted? I get it: you

YOU CAN DO HARD THINGS

might say things are okay, you can count your many blessings, you are good with your normal. But my question for you is this: Are you truly living the life of your dreams? Things remain easy in our comfort zone, and there isn't pressure to grow as a person in your comfort zone. You aren't stretched in your comfort zone, and where is the fulfillment in that? When we excuse ourselves from hard work because we're comfortable, we miss out on opportunities for great things. You might be thinking you are playing it safe with your normal, but I challenge you to take a risk, shatter some glass ceilings, and really go after those dreams that have been tugging at your heart. You can live a good life, or you can live your best life. It won't be comfortable but the work, the blood, sweat, and tears will be so worth the growth and fulfillment that take place.

> **When we excuse ourselves from hard work because we're comfortable, we miss out on opportunities for great things.**

***

Once you have a dream and the vision and determination to put it in action, there is absolutely nothing that you can't do. I have a mantra that I came up with when I began my business five years ago: "See it. Believe it. Pray for it. Work for it." I am where I am because I chose to see, believe, pray for, and work for my goals and dreams. Of these four actions, which are all important, I believe the one most people neglect to do is put in the work.

I recently heard a speaker share that you have to pray and prepare. Wow, think about that. Yes, we have to pray for our dreams and pray that the Lord will bless what we put our hands to, but we have to also prepare. If you want to be a doctor, you have to go to medical school, do your residency, maybe then your fellowship, and it doesn't stop there. You then have to pass board exams to obtain your medical license. You might be praying for God to be with you and lead you all the way through this stressful process. Prayer is powerful; prayer moves the hand of God. However, praying to become a doctor is not enough if you are not also preparing. Preparing is the work involved to bring that dream to life. James 2:17 says, "So also faith by itself, if it does not have works, is dead" (ESV).

Although it is good to get inspired, to have vision like we talked about in the last chapter, there has to be something else that follows that inspiration. That first day in biology class, I could've been inspired to be an A student. I could've prayed and wished longingly for that 4.0, but without taking the necessary steps to work toward that goal, my perfect GPA would've remained simply a wish. In order to push against our sense of comfort, we've got to start working. You have to put in the work; you have to be a person of action.

My favorite definition I found for the word "action" goes like this: **action** is the **accomplishment** of a thing, usually over a **period of time**, in **stages,** or with the possibility of **_repetition_**. First, the good news is this definition tells us that the action leads to an accomplishment! That's where we need vision. We set our sights on what that accomplishment will be. And that gives us hope. At the same time, we cannot ignore that our definition also says accomplishment happens over a period of time, in stages, and with the possibility of repetition. So let's break down what it means to work for our dreams.

1. Accomplishments usually happen over a period of time.

Working toward a goal requires patience. I will definitely say I am not the most patient person on the planet. To be honest, patience is something I majorly struggle with. (Just ask my husband.) I want things right here, right now at this moment. When I was in college and had to take a month to study for exams, I learned patience and discipline. Usually what makes dreams aspirational is the fact that they don't just come naturally to us—they are things we have to work at. We have to put in the time to see the results. I encourage you to be dedicated and patient in accomplishing your goal. Working toward something that doesn't come naturally to you may make you feel weak at first. But be encouraged: It is actually a sign of great strength. Take heart and keep working!

In our culture today, everything is accessible and always at the tip of our fingers. It is very counter-cultural to patiently wait and work for something. We are a culture that is marked by instant gratification. We live in a world where we want instant delivery, same-day shipping, and fast service. Even Chick-Fil-A can have a line of thirty cars yet somehow we still get a hot meal in seven minutes. And how many of us have complained that it took too long? The fact is, we wanted our chicken nuggets yesterday. I will be the first to tell you that my success did not move as fast as that magical drive-thru, but over time, over the days and weeks and months of hard work, I finally was able to take hold of those dreams I envisioned. It takes time, sister. Don't try to fast track your way out of the work.

2. Accomplishments happen in stages.

Part of the industry I work in is working your way up through different ranks. These accomplishments truly take time and happen incrementally. What saved me from getting discouraged early on was knowing I had to move through different levels to see greater success, and that wouldn't happen in just a few weeks. When I began my business, I told myself I was going to give it one year. If I wasn't generating income by that point, I would quit. Another thing I committed to was working towards my goal every day. I didn't start my business and then say, "I will just sit back and see where I am twelve months from now." I committed to put forth effort and work daily! That was crucial for my success. Here I am five years later, and I can tell you that not many people give it one year. They give it barely one month or even one week.

In my industry, you offer products as well as build a team. So, I started alone. No team members, no customers. I had to use the products, then start sharing the products I was passionate about. Then came growing my team. I would have people join me and things were great. I was going forward, and then ouch, someone quit. Oh no, someone else quit. But right then, someone new joined and another and another. It was up and down, filled with highs and lows. All the while, I was planted and determined in my goals. I kept my eyes on my goal, and I knew if I stayed the course—enrolled customers, signed up new team members, and taught them to do the same—I would arrive at the finish line. I would see my dream come to fruition. It didn't matter if days went by and I did not sign up a single customer. I still posted on social media to show my store was open. I still followed up with potential clients. I still did the work and planted seeds. Because when you plant seeds, you will reap the harvest if, and only if, you do not give up. It was always important for me to pause along the way and celebrate the small wins and acknowledge how far I had come. I might not be at my goal, but I am further along than when I started. That perspective always helped continue to drive me forward.

Even as I have grown in my position within the company, I am still signing new team members on. The truth is many of people who join my team each month quit. For a long time, I worried that the problem was me.

WORK FOR IT

Am I a bad leader? Am I not equipping them with what they need? Do they not feel supported? But eventually, I came to the conclusion that of course I can always work to be the best leader I can be, but the decision to set a goal and go after it or throw in the towel and quit is on my team members, not me.

We don't give things up on a whim just in our work or side projects, but in our personal goals too. I read an article that said 80 percent of people who join a gym in January quit within five months Why? Because it takes work. But friends, you know you don't get your bikini bod or six pack overnight. You have to commit and then decide not to quit if you want results. And decide not to quit again next week. And the one after that. I could go on, but I think the point is pretty clear. Our culture wants the results right here, right now, but the accomplishment comes over time. As fast paced as our culture is and as much as we want instant gratification, we have to realize that most, if not all, dreams are going to require commitment and diligent work to see them through.

More than the actual work it takes to start the business, go to the gym, stick to a diet, or write a book is the commitment to keep going. It is not "hard" for me to sit at my desk and type out the words I want to say in my book; it is hard to be disciplined and be committed to doing it every day so that I can complete and finish my book.

It is important to note that while working towards and pursuing your dream, you have to also be flexible and willing to make changes. I run my business primarily online by selling products and a business opportunity. You better believe social media has changed drastically in these past five years, and I've had to adapt the way I work to those new developments. We no longer see posts in chronological order; instead there are now algorithms in place showing you what they think you want to see. It is no longer about quantity and blasting posts all day long! Now, it is about the quality of the post and the engagement you get. Viewers no longer want to be sold to, but they want to connect with you. They say yes to you before they say yes to the products or services you offer. Praise the Lord, social media and I have both evolved over the last five years. I am appalled when Facebook shows me the content I posted years ago. I have to remind myself that what I did back then worked, even though it would no longer work now. I have had to reinvent myself multiple times and evolve with the times, but no matter what changes, consistency and daily commitment to my goals has not changed. I know accomplishments take time, and I am committed to being the person of action who will grow and change right alongside my dreams.

3. Accomplishments require repetition.

Looking back over our definition of action, we've got the ***accomplishment*** of a thing, usually over a ***period of time***, in ***stages,*** and now . . . with the possibility of ***repetition***. Okay, I don't think this will come as a huge surprise to you, but I'll say it anyway. You do not do something one time and *Voila!*, you are an expert and that dream came true.

Hate to break it to you, but I did not post on Instagram once and cash in my big check. Usually, achieving a dream requires doing the same things over and over. I posted photos, stories, personal experiences, customer reviews—I was consistent and I became better at marketing over time. In his book *Outliers*, acclaimed author Malcolm Gladwell argues that it takes 10,000 hours of deliberate work and practice to master something, to become a true expert.[10] Whether or not this theory is true doesn't really matter. What matters to me is knowing that it will take a lot of work, a lot of practice, a lot of preparation to truly be good and successful at something.

> **When we work at things, when we take actions toward our dreams, it is important to reflect on our progress and growth because that helps us stay motivated and propels us forward.**

It is also important to remember that you will not be an expert out of the gate. The repetition of action leads to stages of development. When I was in college, my study habits and time management improved slowly over time. I wasn't always at the same stage I started at; I grew, I improved, I mastered subjects. When we work at things, when we take actions toward our dreams, it is important to reflect on our progress and growth because that helps us

YOU CAN DO HARD THINGS

stay motivated and propels us forward. You don't stop when you are faced with doubt, insecurity, criticism, or fear. You don't stop when what you are doing comes more naturally to someone else. You just keep your eyes on your goal.

***

It's easy to think that all this work would wear a girl out, but I love the promise we are given in Galatians 6:9. "Let us not get tired of doing good, for we will reap at the proper time if we don't give up" (CSB). There are several common reasons that people throw in the towel and tend to quit on their dreams. First, it is taking longer than they thought to reach the goal. Second, it is turning out to be harder than they originally thought. Third, they are tired. I mean think about it. When have you quit something? What was your reason? Sometimes, our goals outweigh our motivation; we want the results, but we don't want to work for it. Other times, we are exhausted by trying hard at something for a really long time.

The number of times I started workout routines and then failed miserably is embarrassing. I once joined a gym determined to work out at least three times a week. I went to Zumba, step class, body flow, and body pump for a good solid month, only to hit snooze on my alarm clock every other day by month two and then by month three, well, you can add my name to the list of the eighty something percent of people who pay but don't use their gym membership. Why did I quit? Well it felt hard, and I didn't have the bikini body after my five classes. I needed to stick with it for five weeks or five months to see the dramatic results I was wanting.

My other downfall is sugar. I love sweets. Like really love sweets. Chocolate, ice cream, cookies, cake, I love it all. I am a very healthy eater despite my minor sugar addiction, but I love me some sweets, and I have loved them since I was a little girl. Every so often, I decide to cut out sugar from my diet. I do fairly well on day one. Day two, it gets hard, and by day three, I change my mind. I give up. The world is not worth living in without sugar. Pathetic, I know. But is it really so hard to stick to this diet change? If I got to the point where I completely eliminated sugar, I bet I would feel better—my abs would look better, my skin would probably even look better. But I am not going to reap the benefits of clean eating while stuffing my face with blueberry donuts.

When all our excuses pile up, or we are worn out or feel like our dreams are too daunting, we must turn to those words from Galatians. "Let us not get tired of doing good, for we will reap at the proper time if we don't give up." Our definition of action fits well with this verse. Action is the accomplishment of a thing over time, in stages, with the possibility of repetition. We could even say, doing good (or achieving your dreams) requires daily commitment that will lead to results in time—if we don't give up.

One way to keep from growing weary is to know exactly what you need to be doing in order to keep working for your dream. Any time I set a goal, I come up with my non-negotiables. I actually write them down so I will stick to them. The key is to identify them so you know what it is that you need to be doing every single day. Then make the decision to be consistent with them. What are five daily tasks that will help you reach your goal? After I made my list, I could not take a day off or a week off. I had to show up daily! I can guarantee if you look deep into the life of anyone who you admire and deem successful, they are consistent with whatever it is that they do! You cannot become an Olympic athlete without training daily, you cannot become a musical artist without practicing, you cannot keep a clean de-cluttered home without tidying up every day. I do not think it is the work itself that is the hardest part to achieve your dream, but the self-discipline it takes to consistently do the work.

When I was in school, my non-negotiables were:

- Always go to class
- Get the dates for the tests for the entire semester
- Record all the lectures
- Come home and review what was taught that day
- Study for at least an hour every day

It was through these disciplined practices of work, of repeated action over time to accomplish a goal, that I walked across that stage with a 4.0 in hand. You have to be self-disciplined to do the tasks to achieve the goal, and you have to know that you will have to give up some good things in order to have the great things. When I

WORK FOR IT

decided I was going to start a business with two little girls both in diapers you better believe there was some work. I made the decision I wanted to be successful, I saw it, I believed it, and I was willing to work for it. And although the work is not the fun part to talk about, it is crucial.

And this is the part I hesitate to tell you. I didn't get to rub the genie lamp, twitch my nose or blink and build a multimillion-dollar business. There was a lot of blood, sweat, and tears involved, and there was a cost to choosing my dreams. I said no to some good things to say yes to some great things. I said no to lots of play-dates with my kids and other moms. I turned down many girls' nights out. I even lost some friends along the way because they didn't understand why I was working so hard at something. I had to give up some really good things. But I did it, I chose to invest into my future and my family's future. I built the business I so badly wanted to build, and I reached the highest rank in my company. With that came financial freedom. My family is now debt free. We were able to build our dream home. I now have the choice to decide where I want to give back, where I want to travel, where I want to send my kids to school. I gained passionate, inspiring friends who I met along the way while building this business. I gave up some good in order to get the great.

YOU CAN DO HARD THINGS

> **THE TRUTH:**
> Achieving dreams takes action and discipline.

We may not all be magical unicorns whose dreams come true overnight, but we can be self-disciplined hard workers and achieve our goals.

You may have to push yourself to step out of your comfort zone. You may have to give up some good in order to get the great. You definitely will have to get rid of some of those time wasters like scrolling through social media or another Netflix series in order to make time for your goal. My guess is that investment will be worth it when you get to check that dream off of your dream board.

You may be comfortable with life right now, but if there is a dream in your heart that you're not pursuing, then you may be sacrificing greatness for the sake of comfort. I don't think there is anything comfortable about living a life with a dream on your heart that you are neglecting to pursue. And I sure as heck do not think you will find comfort when ten years from now, twenty years from now, or thirty years from now, you think back to those dreams you didn't pursue. It is not comfortable living a life of regret. It is not comfortable wondering "What if I ____?" I do not ever want to have to wonder what if. I would rather try and fail forward than not give it a go.

Back when I was in the midst of my quest for a college 4.0, I made some decisions on how I spent my time. John

WORK FOR IT

was on staff as the young adult pastor at our church, so we were always hanging out with the young adults from the ministry. I cannot even count the number of game nights I had to say no to, movies nights I had to turn down, and dinners I had to take a rain check on. I didn't love studying in our apartment on a Friday night, but my dream was worth it. When I proved to myself I was smart, I could get good grades, and I walked across that stage with my diploma, all of the moments and even fun times I missed out on were worth it for this moment for me. Now, this may make absolutely no sense to you. My own husband, to this day, does not understand why graduating with a 4.0 was so important to me. The thing is, it wasn't his dream. It was mine. Your dreams are important to you, and that is what matters. Don't worry about other people understanding them. They don't need to. Even your very own spouse will not care about your dreams like you do.

Your goal may not look like mine. Maybe you want to start a nonprofit, invent something, begin an event planning company, create a makeup line, become an actress, or go back to school. Regardless of the goal, you will find yourself having to give up some good things to achieve the great things. Do not think of this time in your life as a time of sacrifice, because when you sacrifice something, you do not get it back. Instead, think of it as a season of investing, because when you invest well, there will be a return.

The last piece of this whole equation to work for your dream is motivation. No one told me I had to graduate college Magna Cum Laude, but I had a desire from within, and I decided I had to do it. I saw myself doing it and I was willing to commit and give up some good in order to achieve this goal that I deemed great. Because of this, you have to motivate your own self. No one else can do that for you. I cannot expect another human being to motivate me to go after my dreams. How can I think that I can motivate you to go after yours? Sure, I can hope to inspire someone else with my actions. I can even be an example and lead from the front. But motivation? That has to come from inside you. Colossians 3:23 says, "Whatever you do, work at it with all your heart, as working for the Lord, not for human masters." You owe it to yourself to get a little uncomfortable with the areas in life you've settled in. Even more so, you owe it to yourself to give your all in whatever it is that you want to do! Moving from that place of comfort to action will take courage, patience, dedication, and development, but it is so worth it. Go all in, and work for it.

> **Moving from that place of comfort to action will take courage, patience, dedication, and development, but it is so worth it.**

REFLECTION:

What are your non-negotiables? What are five daily things you can do to work toward your goal?

What is something that you've made progress in this year? Celebrate that!

List out some areas where you have possibly settled and become comfortable. Are those comforts getting in the way of going after your dreams?

Chapter 6

YOU CAN RELEASE YOUR PAST

> **THE EXCUSE:**
> If only you knew my past, you'd know
> I don't deserve the life I long for.

My past is riddled with mistakes and missteps. I am disqualified and don't deserve the opportunity to lead others and achieve my goals. How can I move on from what I did or what happened to me when it is part of me and has been part of my identity for so long?

Staring down at the scale, I was horrified by what I saw. I was over my goal weight yet again. *I shouldn't have eaten those extra eggs*, I thought. I need to ask my dad to stop making those. Five pounds over my goal weight, I knew I needed to make some changes. I was nine years old.

I started doing gymnastics and dance at a really young age. When I was in third grade and on team in gymnastics, we would have weigh-ins and goal weights. I also had to keep a food journal and write down what I ate every day.

YOU CAN DO HARD THINGS

My youngest daughter is a competitive gymnast, and thank goodness things have changed. From a young age, I was very conscious of weight; it was something that I focused on and worried about. Then, after my freshman year of high school, I stopped doing dance and gymnastics, and all of a sudden, I started gaining weight.

My sophomore year, I found out that a boy named Brad was saying to another group of boys, "Did you see that SheriLynn got fat?" I was by no means fat in my size four jeans. However, I was a gymnast and dancer who had stopped doing competitive sports, and all of a sudden, my body did change.

Hearing someone else talk about my weight was actually the beginning of years of weight and body image issues for me. Years of starving, binging, purging, diet pills, laxatives, Adderall, and major self-esteem struggles followed. I would live on Diet Coke and one or two pieces of fruit for days at a time. I would try to starve myself. Eventually I would give in, usually late at night, and I would go binge eat an entire box of cereal and whatever else I could find in the refrigerator. I would then feel an overwhelming sense of regret, which would lead to me going to the bathroom, locking the door, turning on the bath tub or sink, and purging what I had binged. It was a vicious, awful cycle. I think my rock bottom was when I was taking ten to twelve diet pills a day, laxatives on top of that, and buying Adderall off of friends in parking lots. I was silently trying to defeat this demon alone. Looking in a mirror, I would hate what I saw. My

RELEASE YOUR PAST

weight would fluctuate because of the way I was abusing and mistreating myself. I can remember crying in bed so many nights, wondering if I would ever get out of this dark hole and be able to look in a mirror and like myself.

It wasn't until Bible College, after years of disordered eating, that I finally got freedom from it. An amazing speaker and author named Lisa Bevere came and spoke to the women's ministry. She prayed over me, and it was so powerful. After that, I started reading Lisa's book *You're Not What You Weigh*. When I finished that book, I started weeping and asked God to set me free from this deep struggle. I was so consumed with food that I thought about it always. I prayed, "God, I'm going to need you to take this idol of food and this obsession with weight." And you know what? He really did. While it was a process, I threw away the diet pills, I started eating healthy, and really tried to make the right choices. I can say, in all honesty, I no longer look in the mirror in disgust, I do not step on a stupid scale dozens of times a day, and I do not starve or binge or purge. I love myself and who God designed me to be.

Now, I look at my daughters, and I would be appalled if my girls were even conscious of their weight. And sometimes, I wonder how I could possibly set a good example for them when, for so many years of my life, I was obsessed with food and my weight. My past tries to hold me back in this way. Can I be a good mom and lead my kids in the right direction when there are so many things I regret from my past? Even in my business, when I'm trying to promote health and wellness, I sometimes

YOU CAN DO HARD THINGS

think: *Who am I to lead this business? I was so unkind to my body for so many years.* I often think that this part of my past disqualifies me, but I have come to learn that it doesn't. I have the opportunity to speak about healing, growth, and battling temptation.

Some of you may be carrying around those painful words that someone said to you. "You're ugly, fat, stupid, worthless, a slut, you can't do _____ . . . " and the list could go on. Hateful words are like daggers that can pierce right through your heart. Whether the past holds loss, betrayal, embarrassment, shame, selfishness, or fear, we all have something in our past that we think disqualifies us from our dreams or the future we want to build. Friends, you cannot let that tragedy, mistake, or old identity keep you down. The past can knock you down. In fact, it will try its hardest to knock you down, but you have to muster up the strength to get up and put one foot in front of the other to keep moving forward.

When life happens, we cope with it in a myriad of ways. Some turn to food as comfort, others self-medicate with alcohol or other destructive substances. You may be one of those who shuts people out and secludes yourself. In all my years of healing, I have learned there are more positive ways to cope with life, like journaling or talking with someone. You may like to work out in order to relieve stress. Some ways of coping are healthier than others. And believe me, it is really important to process the pain of your past and truly work through it. Ignoring past pain, loss, or trauma will not help you move on. Left untouched or unprocessed, the internalized pain will begin showing up and interrupting all areas of your life when you least expect it. We often can equate moving on from past hurt with ignoring it. In fact, when done in a healthy way, moving forward does not mean ignoring what happened in your life; it means taking necessary steps toward your future with the mindset of healing and growth.

An important part of moving forward is forgiving yourself so that you can move on. Even after I started eating healthier and found healing from my eating disorder, I still carried a lot of shame and regret over how I treated my body and let food control me for so long. I held onto that regret in my heart. I didn't forgive myself for the way that this disorder affected my life for many years. One day, I realized that the shame and regret was getting in the way of my growth. While on the surface, my body had moved on from that physical trauma, my heart had not let go of those old ideas I lived by when I was younger. If I tried to keep hiding from my thoughts or avoid facing my shame head on, then I would miss the opportunity to continue healing, growing, and providing comfort to others.

I love that Psalm 103:12 says, "As far as the east is from the west, so far has he removed our transgressions from us." If the Creator of the universe can forgive you and say "What sin?", then how dare we continue to hold on to it? As hard as it is to forgive others who have hurt us, I think it is often hardest to forgive ourselves. We have to learn to forgive ourselves for the mistakes of our past if we want to truly move forward. If we are constantly looking backwards with regret, we are going to miss out on new opportunities and new dreams the Lord wants to birth inside of us for the future.

When I think about the way we hold on to our past, I think about what happens when I take something away from my toddler. Have you ever taken something away from a baby and watched him completely lose his you know what? My son, who just turned one, is obsessed with cords. I'm talking phone charger cords, computer cords, lamp cords, anything with a plug attached to it that could literally electrocute him. What does he do when he gets a cord in his hand? He sticks it straight into his mouth. I always quickly take it away. Now, I am not a mean mom, so I always want to replace it with something good, something better.

> **We have to learn to forgive ourselves for the mistakes of our past if we want to truly move forward.**

As I take away the dangerous, hazardous electrical cord he wants to stick into his mouth, I give him an age-appropriate toy he can play with and enjoy. But like clockwork, every time I take away what could be potentially harmful, he cries. You know the kind of silent cry where their face goes from red to purple and they hold their breath so you have to blow in their face so they will gasp for air and not pass out? That kind of cry. Because he is so upset about me taking something he did not need, he doesn't even realize I gave him something better in return! He is missing out on the new thing right there in his hand because he is focused on what is gone. How many times do we, as grown women, miss out on what God is putting right there in our hand because we are still upset about what we lost in the past? What is in our hand is better, but we have to train ourselves to change our focus and open up our eyes so we can see it.

Moving forward in your life doesn't mean that you block out everything in your past. You want to hold on to the lessons, the things that you learned about yourself, and the people you met along the way. If your mindset is so focused on the future, sometimes you can miss out on lessons from your past or the fullness of the present moment.

Have you ever known a season was coming to an end and it was time to move on? These seasons can feel like you have one foot in the present and the other in the future. A few years after John and I started working at a church in West Texas, we began to have that feeling that it was time for us to move on. We both began praying, and it was confirmed that our season there was done. We felt strongly about moving to Dallas to help with a church plant there. We spoke to the pastor at the church we were at and let him know that we were going to be resigning and moving to help launch this new church. There is nothing wrong with one season ending or one chapter closing and another one starting; that is all a part of life. However, as these next few months of transition began, I felt myself mentally withdrawing from where we were.

YOU CAN DO HARD THINGS

My husband began going back and forth to Dallas, about a five-hour commute, to interview for jobs. During that time, we also began preparing to sell our home and look for another one.

I do not know how to explain it other than I felt my attitude start to change, and I was just ready to move on. I no longer wanted to go to any of the women's ministry meetings at the church because we were going to be moving. I no longer wanted to volunteer in other ministries that needed help. I mean, we were only going to be there a few more months. It was during this time the Lord smacked me upside the head (okay, that's a bit dramatic). It was more like the Lord gently tugged at my heart and said, "Do not forget what is in your hand right now."

Yes, we would be leaving this church and this community, moving to a new city, and helping with a new church, but right now, I was still here int this place. It was a transition time, but there was still a job for me to do. There were still youth group girls that needed to be mentored, there were still so many areas I could serve and help meet a need. There was ministry that needed to be done where I was at.

You may have never been in a transition time going from one church to another, but have you ever missed out on a promotion you felt you so deserved? And then you got so preoccupied with what should have been that you didn't realize all of the opportunities you still had right in front of you? Maybe you applied to a college or program that you did not get accepted into, so now all you want to do is think about what could have been. A serious relationship ended, and you are obsessed with envisioning what your life at age eighty could have looked like with that person. Maybe you are at a job you no longer want to be at, so you are searching for something new. That is fine and dandy, but I encourage you: do not miss out on what is still right there in front of you. Disappointment, changes, and new beginnings are going to happen in life; it's a fact. But even during those times, do not let yourself check out or get too consumed with the "What Ifs" that you miss out on the right now. What is in your hand right now for you to do? Do not let the divine appointments and opportunities the Lord has placed in front of you right now slip away because you want to dwell on the past or focus too much on the future. Seize the moments right here, right now, with what you have been given in this very season.

> **Seize the moments right here, right now, with what you have been given in this very season.**

***

When I think about my own story, I can now look back and see God guiding me to where I am today. He uses all seasons—good, bad, and ugly—to bring joy, redemption, and strength to your life so that you can fulfill the purpose and plan that He has for you.

When I think of taking a tragic situation and using it for the good, I think of my sweet friend Sarah. Her daughter Sadie was diagnosed with leukemia when she was just seven years old. Their lives were turned upside down as they fought this awful cancer diagnosis. Through their journey, Sarah and Sadie began a nonprofit organization. They started Sadie's Sleigh where they would collect toys during Christmas for children in the hospital, and it has since grown to so much more. They have brought awareness to childhood cancer, and I have watched them lobby for more funding for childhood cancer research and advocate for bills to get passed. They have used a tragedy to bring good into the world.

I also think of another sweet friend I have met through my business. She was a former drug addict, and as a teen mom, she found herself living in her parents' basement. Nothing seemed to go in her favor, and every time she tried to stand up, it was as though she would get knocked down again. But instead of staying down, she looked at her daughter and knew she had to rise up. Not only is she still sober, but she started her own business and bought her own home. She is financially able to provide for her daughter, and she is now helping other recovering addicts and teen moms do the same thing! She is proof that your past does not dictate your future.

We will all walk through some bad chapters in our stories. I don't know why painful things happen, but they do. I've come to find that the key to healing is to allow yourself to turn your painful past experiences into powerful testimonies. It isn't fair that you had to walk through a storm, whatever it might have been. It is in the storm where our character is developed. It is in the storm where we experience growth. It is in the storm where we bend but we do not break. And it is in the storm where we find out what we are made of. Romans 8:28 tells us, "And we know that God causes everything to work together for the good of those who love God and are called according to his purpose for them" (NLT). What happened in your past may have not been good, you did not deserve it, and I do not know why it happened. But we have been promised in Romans 8:28 that the Lord will cause it to somehow, someway, work it together for good.

You have probably heard the saying if it doesn't kill you, it makes you stronger. And that is so true. I believe that through every storm, every battle, and every defeat we grow. The pain we experience is inevitable in our growth, but the suffering is a choice. So, you will experience pain as you grow, but you do not have to suffer! It is during some of my lowest points in life that I grew stronger, I developed humility, and I gained wisdom. It wasn't a fun process, but change happened, and I chose to look for the message in the middle of the mess.

***

Shortly after I found healing from my eating disorder, I met John in Bible college when he was visiting his brother who was on staff there. So, the SheriLynn that John knew was in Bible school, going on mission trips, working in soup kitchens, passing out lunches and coats to the homeless, and helping run the children's ministry at church. Just two years prior, I may or may not have been a wild sixteen-year-old with a fake ID sneaking into clubs, running away from home, experimenting with substances that could have most definitely killed me, and doing more than I'm willing to talk about in this book.

When John and I started dating, I knew I had to reveal a little about my past. So, I was trying to find the words to say it all. As I began to confess who I had been before I met him, he interrupted me and said, "I already have an idea, and I don't need to know. You don't need to say anything. Your past is your past." I was stunned. He truly did not care about what kind of past I had.

You would think that knowing that the guy I was falling in love with didn't care a darn lick about my past would be the end of me having to feel any guilt or shame. But there were still times my past would try to rear its ugly head, and I would have to remind myself that it had no bearing on my future. I didn't need to walk around with regret, shame, or guilt. If anyone is in Christ, they are a new creation; the old has gone and the new has come. (2 Corinthians 5:17). If God no longer saw my past, and even my soon-to-be husband was not looking at it, then why on earth would I still dwell on the mistakes I had made? If you have not yet come to realize this truth, then let me be the one to tell you: who you've been does not have to be who you are in the future. The mistakes you have made do not have to repeat themselves again. You have been given a clean slate and a fresh start. If you are willing to move forward, then truly, the sky is the limit. Who do you want to become? What is it that you want to accomplish? Stop letting anything hold you back, especially yourself, and go do whatever it is that you want to do.

> **THE TRUTH:**
> Your past is a part of you, but *hallelujah!*, it's not your present or your future.

We must think forward and set our sights on what is ahead. Your past is just that: your past. It's time to learn from it and move on. It's not who you are anymore! You can use your experiences to lead others to freedom and healing. You are never disqualified from pursuing your dreams.

Looking back on my own life, I wish I had not been bullied in junior high. I wish I did not struggle with learning disabilities. I wish I didn't battle with an eating disorder for years. I wish I had not experimented with all the wrong things in high school to try and fill a void only God could fill. I wish I did not know what it was like to be talked about and even made fun of for starting my own business. These moments were hard. And for much too long, I let them cap off the dreams I thought I deserved. I placed limits on myself because I didn't think I was worth anything more. While I don't love every part of my past, I do love the growth that came and the change that took place in me. Because I've released my grip on the things I held onto for so long, I can share with you my experiences, my stories, in hopes that you can learn from them as well. You can take what you faced and what the enemy wanted to use to bring you down, and instead, you can rise up and dig deep to see what in your story can be used for good. You have a testimony that somebody else needs to hear.

You have a choice. You can stay stuck in your past, with your finger held down on the replay button of that tragedy or that mistake, refusing to let go. Or you can take your finger off of the button, let go, embrace the lessons you learned, and move forward. You can let go of those painful parts of your life and walk in your purpose to go after your dream. Stop trying to figure out "why" things happened the way they did. It is done; it is finished. But don't for one minute think you are powerless. You are anything but that! You have power to change your present situation right now, and you have the power to change your future!

There are two key ideas I've taken hold of to move on from my past: release and embrace. You have to decide how you will respond to failures, tragedies, and mistakes. So many of us hold on tightly to these things, but alternatively, we can loosen our grip and let them go. When we release ourselves from the past, we no longer remain bound by the pain, guilt or shame. Secondly, we have the idea of embrace. One definition of embrace is an act of accepting or supporting something willingly or enthusiastically. You have to embrace the lessons learned, let go, and keep moving forward. I'm not sure if I can say that I have *enthusiastically* accepted everything from my past, but I am to the point where I can *willingly* accept everything from my past. To accept does not mean you are condoning it or saying what happened was okay or right. There are a lot of things that should not have happened in my past. Whether they were things done to me or things I did, I am not saying that they are acceptable. But I can embrace the good, the bad, and the ugly and find a way to use it for good.

> **It takes a warrior to trade in tragedy for a testimony.**

If you have walked through hell and back, I bet you anything that someone needs your story. In order to embrace a difficult past, you have to find even just a trace of silver lining in the midst of it. The fact that you overcame and are still here, sister, that right there is a huge victory! It takes a warrior to trade in tragedy for a testimony. And being able to do that is a huge part of being able to embrace those pieces from your past.

Who knows how many lives you will be able to touch because of your story. So, what are you going to do with your story? Are you going to hold on to it because it is full of pain and keep it for only you? Or are you going to share it so that someone else can learn, grow, find comfort and healing through your struggle? The decision is for you and only you to make. My prayer is that you use your story to help someone else. Take what was meant for bad—that mistake, that heartache, that loss, that pain—and use it for good. That is how you win and come out victorious. Find the beauty in the midst of the ashes.

    Moving forward to embrace your past does not mean that you are pretending like the things in your past didn't happen. The situations that happened absolutely impact and change you. But we get to decide what to do with that impact. We have a say in how we want to use it in our future. That is truly liberating. How can you take what may have been bad and use it for good? Did a situation help you grow? Did it help shape you? Did it show you what you don't want? Did it give you an experience, even a testimony you can share with others? Decide to use it for good! Do not let it define you but let it be a part of your story, let it be a part of the journey of seeing your dreams come to fruition. While we release the baggage of our past and embrace the lessons we learned, we must also embrace the possibilities of the future and the power of our stories. You can let go of the things that have held you back from your dreams for far too long. You can unfog your vision and set your sights on what's ahead, not behind. You can look in the mirror and like who you see. You can love who you are and embrace who you are becoming, past and all.

RELEASE YOUR PAST

REFLECTION:

What is something from your past that you get stuck on?

How have you grown since then? Honor and celebrate the ways that you have grown and moved forward.

Chapter 7

YOU CAN BE ENOUGH

> **THE EXCUSE:**
> Compared to her, I'm not enough.

Everywhere I look, there are women achieving things and doing things that I am not doing. I compare myself to them, and I am left feeling unfulfilled, sad, and even jealous. I get stuck in a place of immobility because I know I will never be the best. I will always compare myself to others and come up short.

Let us now talk about this little aspect of our lives that did not even exist a decade ago . . . Instagram. Truly a blessing and a curse. I am all about social media, and in fact, I built my entire seven-figure business using social media. I love the platform and the possibilities it holds for my business. Social media can be an outlet for creativity, a tool for business, and a way to stay connected to people. But it is also a space that breeds comparison.

We scroll through our newsfeed and see countless celebrities looking flawless. (Never mind the professional hair and makeup they've had done or the filters, presets, and touch ups on each photo.) We see friends who seem to have life figured out; we see entrepreneurs making a name for themselves and building a following. As we come across each perfect picture, our first thought is: *I am not good enough*. Our sweet little photo sharing app has morphed into this sort of dark force to be reckoned with, and it makes sense that millennials are requesting that the number of likes no longer show under each photo. They are tired obsessing over the numbers and want to be rid of the pressure it adds.

Years ago, I had a friend that always left me feeling like I wasn't enough. And just as a disclaimer, this was way back in the days of MySpace. (Anybody remember that?) Each time I saw what she was up to, it was like I just couldn't compete. I felt like whatever I did, she would one-up me, and it was almost like it was intentional. It was draining. I didn't even want to be around her. I was feeling less than, not because of anything she was doing, but because I was comparing myself to her. Then it clicked: the problem was me. So, what did I do as these feelings weighed on me? I prayed! I prayed daily that the Lord would give me love and compassion for this friend. I prayed Psalms 51:10: "Create in me a clean heart, O God; and renew a right spirit within me" (KJV). I was not created to compete with anyone. I am SheriLynn Alcala, no one else. As a practical measure against that spirit of comparison, I stopped looking at her social media account constantly. I stopped always checking

BE ENOUGH

what she was up to while I took time to work on myself. Next, I began to compliment her. I didn't always want to, but when I saw a cute new top she was wearing, instead of thinking, "Man, I wish I had one like that," I would say, "I love your new top; you look so beautiful."

If I felt that kind of comparison when I had to log on to an actual computer to see her MySpace, how much more are we plagued by this constant sizing up when we carry it with us in our pockets all day, every day? Answer: so much more! Friends, we've got to get this under control. First things first: realize that you are seeing a small glimpse of someone's life. Y'all, social media is the highlight reel. It is a glimpse of most peoples' highlights of their day. I have had people say things to me like, "Your family is so perfect!" after seeing me post a photo of my three kids smiling and wearing coordinating outfits. What they didn't see was the twenty-five awful photos on my camera roll, and praise the Lord, there is no recording of me saying things like, "If you do not smile you can kiss TV goodbye today!" or "No! A real smile not a fake smile, girls." Or "I know the sun is bright just close your eyes and open them on three; you won't go blind." I so wish I was joking

> **Stop comparing your real life to someone else's highlight reel.**

right now, but you know I'm not because you've probably done the same thing. Social media is truly a two second snapshot into somebody's day. Stop comparing your real life to someone else's highlight reel. We all have junk. Everyone's kids fight and have snotty noses; mine sure do. I don't think there has ever been a day without tears shed from one of my three kids or myself in my almost eight years of motherhood. My point is this: no one is perfect and no one has it all together. I have yet to meet a mother who says she has found a way to balance her life. We are all just doing our best, the best we know how. Stop comparing your life to strangers on Instagram. We are all real people with real problems.

    I cannot even count the number of times I have scrolled through social media and someone pops up with more followers, more stylish clothes, a more successful business, a more beautiful home, and in a moment, the lie of "She has it all together" crosses my mind. Right then, I have to pause and remind myself that we are not all at the same points in our stories. A helpful saying I often repeat to myself is, "I may be looking at her Chapter 9 when I am on my Chapter 4." And honestly, that is encouraging. Seeing someone else accomplish the same dreams I have shows me that it is possible; I can do it too! I also have to remind myself I was not created to be her; I was created to be me. My life is going to look different. My journey won't necessarily follow the same steps. So when I turn forty and haven't accomplished all the same things in the same order as this person I follow online, I am not bothered in the least. I have been called to reach my sphere of influence. There are people who can relate with me. All I have to do is be the best version of me and

BE ENOUGH

focus on the dreams the Lord has given me.

One of the things about social media and comparison is that we get a peek into people living in different phases of life. I can easily follow someone ten years younger than me and feel bad that I don't look the same as them. Or I can look at someone older than me and wish my kids were more grown up and that I wasn't about to begin potty training baby number three. We are constantly being pulled in directions that distract us from the present circumstances in which we find ourselves. With this in mind, it is important to remember that we are all at different stages in our journeys. You might be looking at someone's mountain top, but you might never see the valley they went through to get there. I also want you to realize that what someone else has and what someone else accomplishes does NOT take anything away from you. Do you realize how liberated you will be when you truly understand that? Seeing your friend succeed does not mean you cannot succeed. Seeing your co-worker get a promotion does not mean you cannot get a promotion too. Seeing your bestie start a blog does not mean you cannot start a blog as well. There is enough for us all!

But be warned, friends: when comparison shows up to the party, its relatives often tag along. Comparison's cousins are jealousy, envy, self-pity, and bitterness. We can experience any one of these with a wide range of thoughts—I am not skinny enough, pretty enough, rich enough, fit enough, happy enough, outgoing enough, organized enough, creative enough, clever enough, adventurous enough, interesting enough. All these thoughts stem from a central lie: I am not good enough as I am now, for who I am in this moment. We compare and compete with one another, and it just isolates us more. Social media traps us alone with this "I'm not good enough" feeling.

So, we try to change ourselves, we work to fit in, we look around and squish ourselves into a mold that doesn't capture who we truly are. We are all guilty of this. This is a side effect of comparison. It seems to me there are some usual paths we take when comparison starts eating away at us. We just give up and feel we can't compete, so we shut down and don't even try to shut out those thoughts. Forget even starting that blog, someone else has a better one. Forget writing that book, a similar one has been written; I missed my chance. It so silly to even type these things but I know I have been guilty of comparing myself to others and then just shutting down and quitting many times before. So what should we do? We need to take the other path. We must learn to break out of the mold and embrace who we are. You do not need to compete or compare; you are enough as you are, right now. We live in a world that needs every single person to be who they were created to be and use the gifts that they uniquely possess. So do not back down, do not give up. Boldly, confidently rise up and be you.

***

Every year at my children's school they have Spirit Week.

BE ENOUGH

It is literally my most stressful week of the year. (And all the other moms can say *AMEN!*) During this week, we have to frantically find these random outfits for our kids to wear to go with the "theme" for each day. I guess this is all in the name of school spirit, but it is basically a week of having to Amazon prime last-minute costumes. We have Decade Day, Crazy Hair Day, Cowboy Day, and last year, we had "Clone Day." During Clone Day, a day where you and a friend or a group of friends dress the same, the majority of kids in Josselyn's class wanted to dress up as Minions. Josselyn, on the other hand, wanted to dress up as a unicorn with her friend Cate. I remember saying, "Josse, almost everyone is going to be a Minion." She looked at me and said, "Mom, you always tell me to be myself, and I feel like a unicorn is more my style. Why do I have to do whatever everyone else is doing?"

    I wish I could sit here and say I applauded my daughter and told her to be a dang unicorn. But I didn't follow my own advice to be confident in yourself, and I sent the poor kid to school as a Minion. I remember picking her up after Clone Day and saying, "Josse, you guys all looked so cute! Weren't you so happy you dressed up as a Minion?" She looked at me and with all sincerity said, "Are you happy, Momma? I really wanted to be a unicorn, but I know you wanted me to be a Minion." Cue total mom guilt and the water works. I looked at her with that pit in my stomach and lump in my throat, feeling almost speechless. I eventually brought myself to say something along the lines of, "I am sorry, baby, next year you can dress up as whatever you want."

Not even realizing it, I was trying to tame my free-spirited, independent, one-of-a-kind daughter and persuade her to be like the majority. I don't want my kids to ever feel like they need to be like anyone else! But there I was, pressured by some outside sense of comparison to others. If I am going to be completely honest, it all stemmed from my own insecurity and feelings of not fitting in with some of the other moms from the school. I wanted to make sure my daughter didn't feel that way. There I was, in my mid-thirties, caring way more about her fitting in than she cared. She was confident, secure, and fine. I, on the other hand, needed to learn a lesson or two from my daughter.

So much of our culture today operates in this tension that we are totally unique yet remarkably just like everyone around us. And I know I have felt the effects of this, as exemplified in my sweet daughter's desire to be a unicorn but ending up a Minion. As we trudge through the constant stream of perfectly curated lives online, showing us how we should look and dress and eat and live, we have to remember that each one of us is so unique, that no one is quite like we are.

There is an amazing TED Talk by Mel Robbins, where she presents research on human DNA and uniqueness.[11] A group of scientists have crunched numbers, factoring in major world events like wars and natural disasters, and the chances of you being born with the DNA you have to the parents you have is approximately a one in four hundred trillion chance.

BE ENOUGH

Even scientists will admit that there was a slim, miraculous chance for you to be born, yet here you are. God knit you together as you for a reason. You are truly a one-of-a-kind, original masterpiece. It is so freeing to know that you were created to be you and only you. And I was created to be me and only me. I can be inspired by someone, I can admire them and learn from them, but I do not have to be them. In fact, I should not try to be them because God created me to be uniquely myself.

There are specific dreams the Lord birthed in my heart that I alone am supposed to carry out. This is exactly why it is so dangerous to fall into the comparison trap. When we get caught up comparing ourselves to someone else, we lose sight of what we are destined to do. Rather than compare yourself to the girl next door, or more realistically, the girl on Instagram whose profile you constantly check, your job is to be the best version of yourself that you can be. So, you get to boldly, unapologetically be you! It can be daunting for me to see what someone else is doing and feel like I could never achieve that. But the thing is I am not supposed to achieve that! It feels overwhelming because I am comparing myself instead of focusing on what I, SheriLynn, was created to do. Try to be inspired by others and know that the success they are achieving in their life is

> **When we get caught up comparing ourselves to someone else, we lose sight of what we are destined to do.**

something we, too, can achieve. But we will only achieve true "success" by being true to ourselves.

When I started my business, I questioned my decision early on because direct sales is not really the "norm" and many people do not understand the industry. I even had some friends say some negative things that caused me to second guess the path I was going down. I had to pause and think about what I wanted and what my dream was. I had fallen in love with some health and wellness products, I loved the culture of the company, and my dream was to go to the very top of it. My dream didn't have to be anyone else's, and quite frankly, I didn't need their approval. This dream was mine. At the end of the day, whether people supported me, cheered me on, or even understood what I was doing did not really matter. This was my dream to pursue for me—and I decided to believe that would be enough. What a tragedy it would have been for me to have let the opinions and thoughts of a few other people rob me from pursuing my dreams.

I love the quote by James Keller that says, "A candle loses nothing by lighting another candle." Someone getting richer isn't taking money out of your bank account, so stop acting like it is! That friend on social media loving her life does not mean you can't love your life too! We can all win, and I truly believe we can all create the life of our dreams. We have to let go of that scarcity mindset. Choosing not to compete and compare helps you be more of yourself. It gives you space and freedom to grow through a mindset of abundance rather than scarcity.

BE ENOUGH

What if we, as powerful, confident individuals, lived with a mentality of enoughness? This mentality enables us to understand that there is enough for us all. We can all win. There is not one bucket of talent, or dreams, or money that we are all pulling from. Stop comparing and looking at what you lack or what you want to change, and celebrate who you are right now. There are enough resources and success for all of us to attain in this world! Comparison and competition are defeated when we live with the correct mentality. Instead of living and thinking out of lack or scarcity, we live and think out of enoughness.

> **THE TRUTH:**
> Your "enoughness" is not measured up next to anyone else.

We must adjust how we speak to ourselves and find our worth not in others, but in God and the identities He's given us. You are enough, and God has given you gifts and abilities to achieve your unique purpose on earth.

When we compare ourselves to other women, we train ourselves to tear each other down and pick each other apart. When we live out of our enoughness, we are quicker to celebrate people around us. When we don't compete or compare, we open opportunities to care for and support one another. There is room at the table for all of us. There is space for all of us to be ourselves.

Celebrating enoughness of both ourselves and other women is a powerful antidote to a culture of comparison. The older I get, the more I understand and appreciate sisterhood and the power of women coming together and linking arms. Imagine if we spent our time encouraging other women in our circle who are chasing their dreams instead of secretly tearing down their efforts behind their back? And don't tell me you aren't guilty of that. If women truly came together and linked arms, I am confident we'd see a dramatic change in our culture.

> Celebrating enoughness of both ourselves and other women is a powerful antidote to a culture of comparison.

The fact is, we live in a male-dominated society. Women with the exact same skill set and qualifications are paid about eighty cents to the one dollar a male makes.[12] In 2019, there were thirty-three female CEOs in the Fortune 500 companies, and that was a 38 percent increase from 2018 when there were only twenty-four female CEOs.[13]

My point is we as women are facing enough struggles just trying to be treated as equals with males in the twenty-first century, and the last thing we need is comparing ourselves to other women on the internet. With that said, why on earth are we wasting our time competing with our sister next to us and wanting what she has? I am a firm believer that we rise by lifting up others. You have a dream tailor-made just for you, so stop looking to the left or right. Her life is her life and your life is yours. Why not cheer on your sister as she runs after her goals while you run after yours?

Living a life of enoughness, I believe, is right in line with the heart of Jesus. When I think of people who feel like they aren't enough or don't have much to offer, I think of the widow who gave her small last two mites. If you read the story in Mark 12:41-44, you can see that Jesus was more pleased with the poor widow's two small coins than the rich who put tons of money into the treasury. Although it may have seemed like the rich gave the most, the widow actually gave more. The wealthy gave out of what they could very well spare, but the widow, on the other hand, gave her whole livelihood despite her poverty. She gave enough. When we bring our gifts to the world, even though they might not feel like much, we are bettering the world through our offering.

I also think of the young boy who offered up his five loaves of bread and two fishes to feed the 5,000. The boy saw a huge need, he met it by giving what he had, and it was blessed by God! It didn't matter that it looked like he did not have much to give to everyone else around him. He still gave it all. He held nothing back. And I also can't help but think of his mom, who would have never thought that the silent work of her momma hands in her kitchen that day would feed a multitude for Jesus. You never ever know what God has planned with even the most seemingly insignificant "somethings" we have to give.

Someone who also used what was in his own hand was David. He was a simple shepherd boy who used a sling and some rocks to defeat a giant long before he was the King of Israel. David was not trying to be like anyone other than himself. He didn't even want to wear Saul's armor to fight the giant Goliath when it was offered to him. He fought his way with his own weapon.

> When we bring our gifts to the world, even though they might not feel like much, we are bettering the world through our offering.

I also think of Moses. He was a runaway with a speech impediment who ended up using a mere staff to part the Red Sea for the Israelites to aid in their escape from Egypt into the promised land. Moses may have not felt like enough, but he was more than enough, imperfections and all.

Mary, the mother of Jesus also comes to my mind. She was young, probably someone easily overlooked in her village, but she had a willing spirit. When the angel of the Lord came to her and told her she would carry the Messiah, she trusted God, even though she had no idea what her future would hold.

That small coin, that lunch of bread and fish, that simple sling, that staff, and that willing spirit may have seemed unimportant and even insignificant at the time. But centuries later, we are still learning lessons from these great people of faith. The widow, the young boy, David,

BE ENOUGH

Moses, and Mary all stepped out in faith and used what they had in their hand to changed their world—and it was more than enough. You might feel small or insignificant, but you are not. You have a world that only you can change! So, open your eyes. Someone—actually many someones—need you and what you have to offer.

You have a sphere of influence right now that you can reach with what you have. Do not miss out on the opportunities and divine appointments right in front of you because you think you have nothing to offer or because you are too busy comparing yourself to others. What the world needs is for you to show up as yourself right now with what you have in your hand. Who knows who will be learning lessons from your story centuries from now?

Understanding enoughness frees us from the constant comparison we live with every day. When you operate out of enoughness, you are happy for that friend who is on that picturesque tropical vacation with her spouse. You can confidently double tap those pictures of your best friend's kitchen remodel even though you have a kitchen renovation on your dream board. You can cheer loudly for that mom who turned her Etsy shop into a full-blown clothing line that is now sold at Nordstrom. You are able to stop comparing, you no longer operate out of insecurity, you have let go of that scarcity mindset, and you realize there is more than enough for us all! That girl on social media living out her dream has not taken away your ability to do the same. How completely freeing it is to live a life knowing that you are enough just as you are.

YOU CAN DO HARD THINGS

What I want you to take from this chapter is that you were created to be you, so own that and be proud of who you are. You have your very own gifts. There are jobs only you can do and people only you can reach. You have a story to tell, and someone out there needs to hear it. So stop hiding, stop thinking you don't have anything to offer, stop trying to be like someone else. Decide today to be the best version of you that you can be. You are more than enough.

REFLECTION:

Are you living more out of abundance or scarcity?

What are some of your gifts?

Chapter 8

YOU CAN TUNE OUT THE CRITICS

> **THE EXCUSE:**
> If I really did what I loved, people would criticize me.

If I pursue my dream, then I'll be more vulnerable to criticism from others. I have more control over what people say about me if I don't publicly follow my dreams, and that way, no one can criticize me.

When I decided to start my business, there were a few people I could not wait tell my exciting news. Yes, I had decided to join a direct sales company, and I was pumped and excited for the endless possibilities. I will never forget sharing with a friend about my decision, and her reply was, "Don't you have a degree in psychology?" I wanted to snap back with, "Yeah but my degree doesn't allow me to stay home with my baby girls and make money!" I bit my tongue instead.

I told another friend about my decision, and her reply was, "I just would never want to be one of those people always trying to sell things to my friends and family." Ouch. All I could think of was, "Would you be saying that if I had opened a clothing boutique or some other kind of brick-and-mortar store?"

After I started quickly moving up the ranks in my company, I had a friend congratulate me. As we were talking, she said, "Enjoy this now because you know these kind of businesses don't last." Excuse me. I just worked my butt off, reached a huge promotion, and you are going to tell me it won't last? What in the living world! I would hope her remark and her criticism was not intentional, but regardless, it caught me completely off guard and was quite painful.

Here is the thing in life I have learned: no matter if it comes to your business, or how you raise your babies, or whatever else it may be, some people will want to criticize you and others will encourage you. You have to learn to tune out the critics, as hard as it is to not let them get to you.

The haters, the critics, the nay-sayers, the Negative Nancys, the Debbie Downers, you know, *those* people. Raise your hand if you can think of that particular person in your life that always lets you know exactly what they think. And when you think of that person, my guess is you also can hear those words they said to you that one time echoing in your head. I'd also bet that you've let those harsh words

TUNE OUT THE CRITICS

define some aspect of your life. Can anybody relate?

If you meet someone who loves criticism, please introduce me, because maybe I have something to learn from them. But in all honesty, criticism from others is one of the biggest roadblocks we have to move past in order to keep following our dreams. So far, we've talked about taking our dreams off the back burner, overcoming fear, cultivating belief and vision, learning to do hard work, and telling ourselves we are enough. Those are all things that we can be working on ourselves so we can stop making excuses and embrace new truths. But when other people start talking to us? When it's outside voices that lead us to make excuses? That's when we need to do some serious thinking about who we are letting define us.

Critics can absolutely affect your belief in yourself and your dreams if you let them. In order to ignore the haters, we need to first identify why we even let the opinions of others affect us. Why do other people's opinions have the power to rock us to our core? It's pretty simple, actually. We want to be liked. We want people to say nice things to us. And we don't want to be told we are doing a bad job. We are people pleasers. We *do* care what others think about us. We naturally want to gain the praises and approval from our circle. I know that phrase "people pleaser" is tossed around a lot, and some people (myself included) are quicker to admit we have a tendency to try and please others above all. But I want to ask you: why should someone else's thoughts, words, or actions toward you rob you of your future?

YOU CAN DO HARD THINGS

This type of approval seeking continues throughout our lives. We want to get good grades, to receive the praises from our parents or teachers, to do well in sports, to show our peers and coaches and bosses we are capable. But all it takes is that one negative comment, that one mean person to say something, and boom, it's like getting the wind knocked out of you. That confidence you had built up for yourself just leaves your body.

***

I can think back throughout my life, and although I've moved on, forgiven, and let go of incidents, I can still see and hear some of the critics from my past that hurt me. I remember when I switched schools going into junior high. I went from a small Christian school to this massive public school. I went from a class of thirty in my grade to a public school with hundreds of other seventh and eighth graders.

I was the new eighth grade kid who was starting a few weeks late into the school year. I literally knew not one soul, and I had no friends. As the weeks passed, I made one "friend," or so I thought. Because I was not in the popular group and she sort of was, she wouldn't eat lunch with me at school. We hung out on the weekends but never at school. This was literally the first time my naive, sheltered self was exposed to this new reality. I had to try to fit in with kids that were quite different than me. After a few days of eating alone, I decided it was more

TUNE OUT THE CRITICS

comfortable and way less embarrassing to eat lunch in a bathroom stall so no one would see me sitting by myself. I ate in the bathroom for the entire year. I remember being so mortified when girls would just come into the bathroom to talk in private. In junior high, a lot of girls liked to have "girl talk" in the bathroom, although I have no idea why. I hoped and prayed each time no one would recognize my blue Airwalks or the hem of my JNCOs from under the stall because I was in there for so long.

So what good could have possibly come from me going through an entire school year without a single true friend? That experience caused me to become an includer. That year allowed me to realize first-hand how painful it is to be left out. I realized how much I limited myself based solely on what other people thought of me. To this day, I have never wanted anyone else to feel that way. And now as a mom, I have made it my mission to teach my daughters to be includers and encouragers. One of my highlights of last year was when Julianna's teacher sent a note home saying how proud she was that Julianna is always helping new students find their way around the school and how she is a friend to all. I do not care if my child is the best athlete, the smartest, or the most liked. I want to raise kind children who are includers.

What we have to realize is that people are people. We are all imperfect beings. There are no perfect people, only a perfect God. You will get mistreated, hurt, let down, and talked about at some point—probably numerous times in your life. That is a fact. But what you can control is how

YOU CAN DO HARD THINGS

you treat others and how you respond when others treat you poorly.

***

More recently, I faced some criticism when I started my business in 2014. The flood gates opened with the nay-sayers. *SheriLynn Alcala is doing one of those pyramid schemes, SheriLynn has veered off from the calling God had on her life. SheriLynn's posts are so annoying.* Isn't it funny that people think they know more than our Creator about our calling? I was talked about, unfriended, and unfollowed—all because the haters didn't like my new business. I was being criticized for working to change my family's financial situation and really change my family's legacy. But because these people outside my close circle didn't understand what I was doing, they were going to bash it. Did I let it get to me? Well for maybe 2.1 seconds, but thankfully, at thirty years old, I had grown, matured, and realized that criticism was just a part of life. I did see who my true friends were during it all. I saw who were the ones who supported me, asked me how everything was going, and really genuinely cared to hear about what I was doing.

And you know what? As time went on, I started to succeed. Within my first year, I jumped into the Top 100 income earners out of over 100,000 reps globally. Then the next year, I jumped up to being one of the Top 10 income earners globally, and since then I have stayed in the Top 10

TUNE OUT THE CRITICS

of the company. Not only did I achieve those milestones, but so many other women from my team are also top income earners. You would think the success of not only me but also my team would silence the haters. But the critics are going to talk about you regardless of the facts.

In my business, I cannot count the number of women who join my team and then quit within a week or two because of something someone says. "My mom said she had a friend, cousin, aunt, neighbor who tried that industry and it didn't work." Or "My best friend said she thinks it's annoying when I post about my business or products on Facebook, so I don't want to post anymore." How sad that they let someone else's thoughts and opinions control what they do.

In this world, it doesn't matter if you are doing right or wrong . . . you will be criticized. Actually, even if you do nothing, you will be criticized. *She works too hard. She doesn't work enough. She gave up her career for her kids.* Blah. Blah. Blah. If I let those other voices stop me or cause me to quit, what good would that do? I will never be able to please everyone, and that is okay. If we know that criticism is a force that comes up against us—regardless of if we succeed or fail—what do we do with it? How can we master it? I want to look at a few different ways that we can stop letting criticism be our excuse.

First, identify who your critics are. Your critic may be a family member, spouse, maybe even a parent, close friend, peer, or just some jealous troll on social media. If your critic is actually your mom or maybe a sister or best friend, then that can be a little tougher to navigate. Yes, even friends can be critics. So how do we deal with that? I don't want you to instinctively punch right back when someone throws some harsh words at you, but I do think there is a little sprinkle of healthy conflict and conversation that you can initiate. You are going to have to just have a "Let's be real" moment and say, "Hey I am trying to live a life of gratitude and be positive; do you want to join me in doing that?" Or "Hey these are my goals and dreams; can you please support me in them?" Sometimes, setting boundaries in your close relationships with people is the most loving thing you can do. If they can't get on board with your dreams, then set some boundaries as to what they can talk to you about. It may or may not help, but regardless, you need to realize that you have to guard your mind and guard your heart against these types of people.

And I will be honest: It stinks people are like that. It really does. But you know what? Even Jesus had haters! I mean, the man could walk on water. He is the Son of God. He loved on, ate with, and stood up for the outcasts, the poor, and the sinners. Yet somehow, even He was criticized, talked about, judged, and hated. If Jesus, who was perfect, was not exempt from haters, then what would make us believe that we would be exempt? As a perfectionist, this is a huge relief to me. I think sometimes we equate perfection with not having conflict, but that just isn't true.

Once we have identified what critical voices we are letting define us, we have to have a reality check. The next thing you have to do is realize that other peoples' opinions

TUNE OUT THE CRITICS

have nothing to do with who you are, where you are going, or how you view yourself. Yes, it feels good to win approval and get praises from others, and yes, it hurts to be criticized and talked about. You have to remember that not one single critic should have the power to slow you down, stop you, or make you second guess for a moment what you have set out to do. Those dreams, ideas, goals, visions were birthed in your heart for a reason. They are yours, not your Instagram followers'. I believe the Lord placed those dreams inside you for such a time as this. I also believe what the Bible says in John 10:10, "The thief comes only to steal and kill and destroy . . ." So, the Enemy is out to destroy you and your dreams! But no one, and I mean no one, should have the power to rob you of your destiny.

When you name your critics and properly situate them among the chorus of other voices we hear on a regular basis, the harsh words quiet down. Only then can we begin to focus in on the voices that matter most.

THE TRUTH:
Let your truth be louder than any other voice.

Even Jesus had critics. Don't let critics stop you from pursuing your dream. Listen and trust yourself. Trust your intuition. Trust God's plan for your life. Don't let the opinions of others cause you to shrink your dreams. Let your success speak for itself and silence their criticism, and find the voices that cheer you on.

YOU CAN DO HARD THINGS

My oldest daughter is a great little basketball player. Yes, the same daughter I started a business for so I could pay for dance classes took more after her father and likes to dribble more than plié. It blows my mind that when kids are only seven and eight years old, the parents in the stands at the basketball games get loud, crazy, and even mad when they think the referee made a wrong call. They yell when one of the players didn't pass the ball like they should have or when someone misses a shot. If you happened to wander into that gym, you would think we were at a WNBA game, not a second grade recreational game. One heated game in particular, I started to listen to the chatter of the other parents in the stands. It got me thinking: if Josselyn continues to pursue basketball, which I am most certain she will, these games are only going to get even more intense. (Lord help me!) As that happens, she is going to have to learn to not let the sideline commentary distract her from playing the game. Even more importantly, she cannot let those voices from the crowd turn into voices in her head. She could easily start to believe that she's not as good of a player if she took any of those harsh words to heart.

I recently read a book by Brené Brown called *Daring Greatly*.[14] This whole book is based off a quote by Theodore Roosevelt that caused Brené to rethink the shame and criticism she internalized. This one quote made her examine what kept her from dreaming big and daring greatly. Doesn't that seem fitting for what we're talking about? To not be defined by others and to learn what we're

TUNE OUT THE CRITICS

really made of. If you haven't seen this quote before, I want you to take a minute and sit with it. Mr. Roosevelt says:

> *It is not the critic who counts; not the man who points out how the strong man stumbles, or where the doer of deeds could have done them better. The credit belongs to the man who is actually in the arena, whose face is marred by dust and sweat and blood; who strives valiantly; who errs, who comes short again and again, because there is no effort without error and shortcoming; but who does actually strive to do the deeds; who knows great enthusiasms, the great devotions; who spends himself in a worthy cause; who at the best knows in the end the triumph of high achievement, and who at the worst, if he fails, at least fails while daring greatly, so that his place shall never be with those cold and timid souls who neither know victory nor defeat.*[15]

I mean, don't you love that? If ever in my life I say something a teaspoon of that poetic and moving, I will feel very accomplished. I guess we can say this book you're reading is my best go for now! But let's break this down. The basic premise of what both Brené and our friend Teddy are saying is this: the critic doesn't count. And perhaps more importantly, they tell us the voice that matters is the one that is in the arena. Your voice. Not the people in the stands that don't know the stakes of your dream. If those voices aren't the ones that matter, then we

YOU CAN DO HARD THINGS

need to tune our ear to the right voices. Criticism taken to heart makes you want to sit down or quit trying or shrink your dreams to where they're at least manageable enough. But look back at our Roosevelt quote and picture yourself: The credit belongs to the woman who is actually in the arena, whose face is marred by dust and sweat and blood; who strives valiantly; who errs, who comes short again and again. Credit belongs to the woman who is chasing her dream, who picks herself up when she fails forward, who tries hard and believes she can do hard things.

What I want you to take hold of, friend, is that part of dreaming big, part of taking down those excuses of criticism means learning to strive valiantly in spite of the critic. And yes, that probably means you'll face some shortcomings or get a little scraped up. It means you have to have those tougher conversations with people you love. And even if you fail, even if, at least you fail while daring greatly and dreaming anyway. Those people in the stands? They don't know just how much is at stake.

> **Credit belongs to the woman who is chasing her dream, who picks herself up when she fails forward, who tries hard and believes she can do hard things.**

I think back to Josselyn on that basketball court. Words of both encouragement and criticism flying around that gym. She's working hard, running up and down the court, trying to stay focused on the game. And I hope and pray I'm training her to hear the right voices. First, to know her own, to trust her instinct and play the game well. But second, I want her to hear those voices in the crowd cheering so loud that they drown out all the others. Me, her dad, her sister, her brother. Truth is, just as much as I remember the words of criticism from people who tried to hold me back, I also remember and cherish dearly the words of encouragement from those who love me and cheer me on. Because praise God, not everyone is a hater!

We are going to spend more time in the next chapter talking about finding your tribe of friends, but I just want to say up front that I am not so pessimistic as to think that everyone I meet is going to be critical of me. This is a great aspect of our truth this chapter. If being afraid of criticism has kept you from doing what you love or what you hope to do, it is time to adjust the dials and tune into a different station. As you embrace the truth that the critic's voice isn't the one that counts, I hope you will find the voices that cheer you on, and stick with them!

YOU CAN DO HARD THINGS

REFLECTION:

How do you respond to criticism naturally?
Do you shrink back?

What have you let take you out of the arena?

Practice saying your truth, the truth about who you are, what you are capable of, and what you can accomplish out loud to yourself.

Chapter 9

YOU CAN FIND YOUR PEOPLE

> **THE EXCUSE:**
> Life will be easier if I go it alone—there's less chance of getting hurt.

Friendships are exhausting and challenging. I've been burned too many times in the past and it's hard for me to open up to people. Life will be easier if I do it alone. Plus, I have so much going on that I really don't have time for friendships. Community would be nice, but I don't need it.

When John and I were first married, we lived in the small town of Midland, Texas. John grew up there, so he had friends from high school that were still around. I, on the other hand, was needing some community. More than that, I needed friends. Some of John's friends were also newly married, so we started to hang out with them and their wives. I really liked these girls. They came from a different social circle than me: West Texas oil and gas money. They were debutants (for the record, I had

YOU CAN DO HARD THINGS

to Google what a debutant even was). They had huge, gorgeous homes even as newlyweds. And well, John and I were in that 500-square-foot apartment. They wore designer everything, and I was more of a Target girl.

These girls seemed nice, and I so badly wanted some other married friends. So, I worked really hard to try to fit in and be accepted by these girls. Sometimes it meant buying something I couldn't afford so I wouldn't be embarrassed by not spending money when they were going on shopping sprees. I would buy a couple things, enough to not draw any attention to myself like I would have if I'd bought nothing. A day or two later, I would go back to return the items I couldn't afford. I wanted to fit in, as silly and ridiculous as that sounds.

One day, three of us wives were going to have lunch and go shopping. One of the girls said she was going to text me in the morning when and where to meet. I waited and waited. I even texted her but received no response. A little later that day, John told me he was going to go golfing with these girls' husbands. Finally around 3:00 p.m., one of the girls texted me and said she was sorry she hadn't texted, but she ended up having lunch and hanging out with her husband. I was so confused, because John told me he was golfing with her husband hours ago. There had to be some sort of mix up. I texted John to confirm who he was golfing with, and yes, it was, in fact, her husband. John even sent me a nice photo of them on the course making silly faces. My stomach dropped, and I knew she had intentionally lied to me. For whatever reason, she didn't want to hang out with me. When John got home, he said that after we hung up, his buddy got a phone call from his wife, and she was furious at him for some reason. I bet I know why.

The guys had already planned for us to all go to dinner that evening. Her cover was blown, and now she'd have to sit through a meal with me. I'll shoot you straight: that was, without a doubt, the most awkward triple dinner date night of my life. As I replayed the event and tried to understand it, I started to think of a few other times the girls and I had planned outings and I was never told when or where to meet. I had thought they were just accidents, but that day, I saw the truth as it was. These mean girls didn't want to be my friend. I didn't fit what they had in mind. They had a bad habit of gossiping and talking about other girls I didn't know, and I had a sinking suspicion this was the same way they probably talked about me.

This was the end of me trying to befriend these not-so-nice girls. I released myself from that unhealthy "friendship," but I was left with little lies about myself floating in my head. I didn't have enough money, wasn't trendy enough, wasn't "high society" enough, wasn't worth spending time with. I started believing John and I were doomed from having couple friends we would actually enjoy being with—and more importantly, I was afraid we wouldn't find friends who would care to invest in us.

Have you experienced this before? Maybe you moved to a town where you knew a few couples, but were disappointed they never initiated any gatherings. Or you put yourself out there to a new friend, only to feel like being yourself wasn't quite enough for them. Maybe there was a group you really wanted to be a part of, but time and time again, you felt excluded and uninvited. Maybe someone was just plain mean to you. Here's the thing: there are mean girls out there. It's a sad, unfortunate truth. And just as those girls hurt me, I know I have hurt others girls in my life as well. Perhaps not intentionally, but I have done it. Imagine for a moment, though, if I let that one experience scar me and make me think all women are evil and therefore, I should shut myself off from anyone who tried to be my friend for all eternity. That would be absurd.

Just like our excuse at the beginning of the chapter says: we start to think that things might just be a little easier if we didn't let anyone in. We could avoid the hurt of the messy friendships. We could just hunker down in our houses like it's the apocalypse and not worry about seeing anyone except our husbands and children. Life will be easier alone. I had all those thoughts for a while when John and I were trying to find our footing as a couple. I looked at older couples at our church that had dear friends who were as close as family. I saw women that raised children together, supported each other, loved each other. And I believed that because I had been hurt, I was now out of the friendship running.

Now when these old thoughts creep back in, the lie detector in my brain starts to go off, and I know those old untruths and excuses are trying to gain some ground. My guess is you wrestle with some of these same challenges when it comes to friends. I want to put a name to some of these lies and talk through how we can combat them with the truth about friendship.

Lie #1:
We think that we can do life alone.

There is a reason Proverbs 27:17 says, "As iron sharpens iron, so one person sharpens another." This verse makes me think of my set of kitchen knives. Hang with me. At first, the knife you got on your wedding registry works fabulously on its own. Sharp, swift, efficient, powerful. But you know how knives are: they are used every day, they add other tiny knives to their set, they're busy cooking for the family, making preparations for daily sustenance or if you are like me, you use them more often to open Amazon boxes than to actually meal prep. And if you use a knife over and over, it starts to dull. It doesn't work as well as it should if it doesn't get sharpened. In order to sharpen it, you have to use that long steel rod that comes with the set that you otherwise do not know how to use. And so I have learned (most likely via the internet) that you actually have to put the knife in contact with other metal in order to sharpen up the blade. In that back and forth of the knife and the sharpener, the blade gets refined, renewed, and restored to do what it is fully capable of doing.

Maybe my analogy is a little on the nose, but I want to

demonstrate just how much wisdom is in our verse in Proverbs. It's like King Solomon was cluing us in on something essential about our own flourishing: doing things alone just won't cut it forever. I know we hear this verse a lot, but in practical terms, when we think about kitchen knives, we can better understand what happens to us when we don't let ourselves be sharpened by others. When we do not have the right type of iron-sharpens-iron people around us, we will naturally get tired, weary, worn out, and dull over time—especially when we are pursuing our dreams. The truth is, we need strong friends that will sharpen us when we rub shoulders with them. We need friends who aren't afraid to be in real contact with us and our circumstances, friends who want us to be our best and sharpest selves.

> **The truth is, we need strong friends that will sharpen us when we rub shoulders with them.**

Lie #2:
If I trust another woman, I will get hurt.

We avoid female relationships because we have been burned in the past. Maybe you were betrayed, talked about, judged, or mistreated by a supposed girlfriend or group of girls. After those girls in Midland made it clear I wasn't going to be their friend, I was wary of girlfriends altogether. I mean, how many times have you heard girls say they just get along with males better than females. Women have been listening to that lie since, gosh, maybe junior high.

About two weeks after that incident, John had another buddy move back to Midland with his wife. I remember thinking: *Oh no, here we go again. I just can't live up to these Texas girls.* We met up with the couple, and lo and behold, this new girl was actually from California like me. Hallelujah! This whole West Texas oil and gas world was going to be new to her as well. We ended up having dinner, and she and I just clicked. She was the sweetest, funniest, most God-loving girl ever. She had a heart of gold, and our friendship began that night. And thirteen years later, she is still one of my very best friends. Through thick and thin, we have been by each other's side. We have walked through pregnancies, health scares, marriage problems, deaths, starting businesses, and so many other critical, pivotal moments of life together. Praise God I didn't keep believing the lie that all women were out to get me. I am so glad that being burned by a couple so-called friends didn't keep me from wanting to get to know the new friend who turned out to be an answer to prayer.

Lie #3:
I don't have time for friends.

The last lie I think we believe when it comes to finding friends is that we don't have time for girlfriends. Raise your hand if you have a few of these items on your

YOU CAN DO HARD THINGS

calendar: school, work, dating, kids, grandkids, husbands, volunteering, church, extracurricular activities, working out, pursuing that hobby, building businesses . . . The list could go on and on. But even in the midst of all the chaos, don't you still want support? Don't you still want community? Don't you still want to be inspired?

What I have learned is that all kinds of relationships require effort. Different seasons in life are busier than others, but when it is all said and done, we make time for what is important. If I were you, I would take a look at your friendships. Which of those relationships help you grow and help you be a better version of yourself? The ones that are uplifting and inspire you and challenge you to be better—make time for them! Those fake, superficial ones that you know aren't true and authentic, by all means, let those go. I have girlfriends who I maybe see once a month, if that, but when we finally get together at our favorite breakfast spot, it is like no time has passed at all, and I always leave feeling so refreshed. I'm in the baby raising stage of my life. Long hours, countless items on my schedule trying to keep my three small humans alive, and I know I would be a hot mess without my girlfriends. They are worth me rearranging my schedule to make some time to get together. Don't devalue the importance of even just a little time with a few good friends.

> **Don't devalue the importance of even just a little time with a few good friends.**

FIND YOUR PEOPLE

> **THE TRUTH:**
> You can't pursue your dreams alone.

We must go after our dreams, and in order to do so, we must have support. There are women out there who will cheer you on and lift you up. You can be a wife, mother, and business owner, and have wonderful friends!

Have you ever heard the statement that you are the average of the five people you spend the most time with? I believe this is so powerful and so true. Whether we want to admit it or not, we are influenced by the people we surround ourselves with on a regular basis. So, ask yourself right now who are the people you are becoming like? Are they positive people who encourage, uplift, and challenge you to be better? Or are they small-minded, negative people who just want to put out your fire?

There have been numerous times in my life where I had had to stop and look around at who those five people are that I have been spending my time with. Are they the kind of people I want to be like? Do I walk away refreshed after we spend time together? Is it a two-way friendship? Do they support my dreams and cheer me on? Are they the iron-sharpens-iron type of friends? If the answer is no, I always make some changes.

For years, I had this friend. I would have even called her a best friend. Every year for her birthday I planned her party. Even when we weren't in the same city, I would send gifts. I was the one always calling her to hang out; I was the one always checking in on her. Now that I look back, all of our conversations always revolved around her, her life, and her problems. I tried so hard to support her and always be a good friend. When my husband would point out the relationship was always me giving, I would make excuses for her. *She was guarded because of her upbringing, she had a hard time letting people in, she really did love me, I was her best friend,* I would say. But even after she moved, it was me trying to text and call her to stay in touch, me giving a lot to her and receiving very little—or often nothing—in return. This was a one-way friendship. I had some hurt I had to work through, but finally I had a come-to-Jesus moment. I realized that wasn't a true friendship. It wasn't healthy for me to care so much when she didn't even try to keep the friendship, so I had to make the hard choice of letting go. Does that mean that I don't love her? No, I love her and her family. But I had to let go of an unhealthy friendship.

 I have also had to do this was negative relationships. I had a girlfriend I met early in my business who I really liked! We clicked and connected. It was fun having someone who understood the line of work I was in. The relationship started out great. We would bounce ideas off of each other and inspire one another. I truly valued my time with her, and I made it a priority to get together with her. As time went on something changed. Her positivity turned to negativity.

 She became negative about anything and everything

that had to do with business. I found myself working so hard to speak life and positivity into her. I tried to change her perspective. I would leave an hour-long lunch and feel drained. It didn't take long for her negativity to rub off on me. All of a sudden, I found myself agreeing with her and feeling the same way. Once again, my husband spoke some truth into my life which opened my eyes. This was no longer a healthy relationship. It didn't mean I did not still love this friend, but I had to set boundaries. I could not continue to spend time with someone who was going to bring me down.

***

Over my years of trying and failing at friendship, I've come to believe that friends are both difficult and worthwhile. As hard as it is to be hurt by friends, to give more than we get, to be brought down by negative people, the beauty and power of true friends outweighs the struggles.

So will you get hurt? Yes, I can almost guarantee it. But more important than the negative experiences are the positive ones! I have so many real, authentic, uplifting, girlfriends in my life. These are the kind of women who cheer me on, not ones who wait for me to fail. They encourage me to dream big and reach for the stars; they don't criticize me or make fun of my dreams. There are way more nice girls out there than mean girls, I promise. And you deserve to have true friends to walk through life with. But first, you have to take your guard down and be open to letting people in. It's risky, yes, but it is 100 percent worth it. We were not created to live this life alone. We need friends in our life. Friends say, "Don't go alone, let me go with you." Friends say, "I see that you are vulnerable and in possible danger; don't worry I have your back. No one is going to get you while you're down." And friends say, "Not only will I go to battle for you, but I will watch out for your kids as if they were my own."

I would not be where I am today in my business, even in my life, without some absolutely amazing iron-sharpens-iron women. I am a firm believer that no one cares for your dreams like you do, but let me tell you that there is nothing quite like the support of a friend who believes in you and your dreams. My sister-in-law Stacey is truly my best friend. She is the big sister I always wanted and an answer to prayer. (A fun fact is that she actually introduced me to my husband when we were in Bible school together.) Anyways, every single week I get a text message or a voice memo from her speaking life over me. She says things like, "SheriLynn, I am praying for you today. You are an amazing mother and wife, and a world changer." She literally does this every week, on Tuesdays to be exact. She believes in me and my crazy, grandiose dreams. She supports me, and you know what? Every time I listen to her voice memos or read her texts, my belief in myself grows just a little.

There are times I have had a rough day, when things are not going how I would like. I have an unhappy customer, John has to work late, the girls have after school activities at the exact same time in two different places, and I am trying to working towards a promotion that seems pretty far-fetched. In those hard moments, when life gets chaotic, when that goal or dream feels pretty impossible, sometimes you just have to borrow that belief from a friend. In my case, my sister-in-law believes in me and believes I can do hard things. When I don't have enough belief on my own, I know I can draw from the belief she has in me. Borrowed belief can get you through some pretty hard times.

Seek people who believe in you and believe in your dreams. Seek friends who are bigger dreamers than you. Seek friends who are quick to encourage and uplift you. It is in these friendships where you will be sharpened and become more confident and focused in achieving your dreams.

We need to completely ditch the excuse we can do things alone. When we try to navigate life on our own, we miss the chance to be sharpened and refined by other brilliant, wonderful people. I never want to be the biggest dreamer in my circle; I never want to be the smartest person in my tribe; I never want to be the most successful amongst my friends. I don't want to continually be the only one pouring into a relationship. I want to surround myself with people who challenge me to be better, reach higher, and do more. And in return, I want to be the kind

> **Borrowed belief can get you through some pretty hard times.**

of person that inspires others. Stop thinking you have to walk through life alone. Stop thinking everyone is going to hurt you. Stop thinking you are too busy for friendships. Stop spending time with people who don't lift you up. Level up, my friend, and find a good, solid, uplifting tribe to do life with. Find people who encourage you in your bold, crazy, God-sized dreams. Find people who support you when you have a dream. Find people with open minds and big hearts.

REFLECTION:

Which of the lies about friendship do you find yourself believing? That you can do life alone, that friends will hurt you, or that you don't have time for friends? Write down the truths you're learning instead.

Do a little friend evaluation in your life. Life can be so chaotic at times, so write down the names of a few of those good friends you can always count on. In the midst of all the things going on, make an effort to pick up the phone and call one. Try to meet for coffee, have a play date with your kids, meet for a quick bite to eat after work. What you might need right now is just thirty minutes of adult interaction with a friend.

YOU CAN DO HARD THINGS

If you need a friend, join a small group at your church, get involved in a Bible study, check out your local MOPS group if you have young kids, or even build some friendships within an online community. I have done all of the above, and so can you. Write down your first step towards finding those friends!

Lastly, I want you to do one more evaluation and ask yourself if there are some people in your community that maybe shouldn't be in there. I truly believe we are supposed to love our enemies and pray for those who hurt us. However, we are also told to be wise and use wisdom. If there are some unhealthy or toxic relationships in your life that you need to protect yourself against, then do it.

Chapter 10
YOU CAN SAY NO

> **THE EXCUSE:**
> I'm too busy.

You won't believe how busy I am. I am responsible for so many things, so my dreams can wait. My calendar is full of activities, my plate is overflowing. I can't do anything that's just for me; that's too indulgent.

I use to think it was not ever okay to say no. If I was asked to be room mom for one of my girls' classes, I would say yes. Host a Bible study? Absolutely. Be a chair on a committee in Junior League? What the heck, sure! Lead a table in my MOPS group? Of course. Host that baby shower, wedding shower, any other shower? You got it; I love showers. Be on the greeting team at church? Welcome! Start a new business endeavor? Yes and amen.

Now, those things are all great! In fact, I thoroughly enjoy doing them all. But I am only one person. And I also have a minorly important role as wife to John and mother to my three little children. Maybe I have some prioritizing to do . . .

The first year I started my business, it was hard. I worked a ton, and I was a stay-at-home mom taking care of my girls. I was also the women's ministry director at our church, and I helped my husband with the young adult ministry he ran. A few months after beginning my business, my oldest daughter started a two-day-a-week preschool. At this point, I was barely surviving the early days of my business and growing my team, yet for some reason I signed up to be the room mom for her class. I now realize I made this hasty choice out of mom guilt. I felt bad I was working, so I thought I needed to overcompensate for it by doing more. (Why do we as women do this? I have never seen my husband feel guilty about going to work too much, and therefore, feel the need to sign up to make twenty pumpkin pies for the fall festival.) Well, my room-mom role meant I planned all of the class parties, and for the room full of three-year-olds, everything is a party. Let's just say, I was in over my head. That year was pure chaos. Starting a business while parenting young children is hard enough, but when you add all the other things to my plate, I was unable to keep up.

One Thursday in particular is burned into my memory. I walked up to the class to pick up my three-year-old from preschool and saw the room filled with parents. I was so confused. The door was open, and every child had a mother or father with them. Everyone except my daughter. I looked at the teacher and said, "What is going on?" She had this

SAY NO

surprised, confused look on her face and said, "Today is our end-of-year class party." I thought, Wait . . . it can't be. It's next week, and I am the room mom. I AM THE ROOM MOM! I mean, why would you not have the end-of-year party on the last day of school? But that is beside the point. Did I write it down wrong in my calendar? Did they give me the wrong date?

The truth was, I had just forgotten. At home sat all the cute summer-themed plates, napkins, and décor I had purchased for the party. I had crafts and party favors for every child in bags in my pantry. I even had the ice cream and sprinkles for the sundaes the kids were going to make, and none of that stuff was with me! I missed the entire ordeal. My face felt hot, my chest was pounding, and I did everything I could to hold back the tears as I apologized. The teacher told me not to worry and that another class had shared some ice cream with them. Here is the nail in my coffin: they had some white paper plates and paper towels—shoot me now! Plain plates! Paper towels! Oh, my heart.

I stood there for five minutes as everyone began to pack up their child and their belongs, and then I grabbed my daughter and almost sprinted to my car while pushing my stroller which had my two-year-old in it. The moment my car door slammed shut, I lost it—like fully lost it. Just imagine the world's worst ugly cry with snot flying everywhere along with hyperventilating. Yes, I'm talking about me, not my toddlers. It was then I realized I was just in over my head with life. I wanted to do it all, but I just couldn't.

YOU CAN DO HARD THINGS

As bad as I wanted to be Superwoman, Supermom, Super Business Owner, I was a human and could only carry so much. I started to replay the last few months in my head. I saw myself losing my patience with my girls, getting mad constantly at John, getting overwhelmed about everything, and just not enjoying my life. I know that there are going to be busy seasons in life, and there are tons of things that we have to do that are absolutely non-negotiables. But there are also times where we voluntarily overload our plates or maybe get guilt tripped into taking on way too much. I was so overcommitted that my kids were not getting a good version of me, and my husband was certainly not getting a good version of me. I am not sure what I was trying to prove or to who I was trying to prove it, but the version of me that resulted from trying so hard was not pretty.

> **Every time I said yes to something, I was essentially saying no to something else.**

And just like that, after the emotional breakdown in my car in the pre-school parking lot, I changed. I really, honestly, truthfully changed. I decided I had to take a look at my life, come up with my priorities, figure out what it was that I wanted to do, and then do those things well. Every time I said yes to something, I was essentially saying no to something else.

Everyone is different, so this may or may not resonate with you. For whatever reason, when I am "busy" or "working," I think I am being productive. But busyness does not equal productivity, especially if you are busy doing tasks that have absolutely nothing to do with your dream or goal. Let me go on to say that busyness is not a good indicator of success either. Stop right now and think of the things you are "busy" doing all day long. Are any of those things helping you get closer to that goal you have? I understand if you are anything like me and are in this baby-raising season of life, a lot of the things on your to-do list or calendar involve your children. Taking them to and from school, after school activities, basketball practice, soccer, cheer, dance, Girl Scouts, music lessons . . . the list is never ending. You might be taking care of an infant, so your list involves feedings, burping, changing diapers, rocking to sleep, and then repeat. Some of you are working a nine-to-five job and killing it in the corporate world. You are at work, then come home to your kids, do dinner, the whole bed time thing, and then you are up before it is even light out the next morning to do it all again.

So much of what we do in these seasons are non-negotiables. In many ways, our packed calendars feel inevitable or even necessary. But look closely. Are there things in there, roles or duties you have committed to, that are not essential and are not helping you get even one step closer to your goal? Are there time wasters in your schedule right now? Are there things that are good but are not serving you or your current dream right now in this season? If so, those things have to go. Being busy does not equal being successful. And as I have said before, sometimes we give up good things to get the great things.

It is also crucial to look at where your time is going and see if you are wasting any of it. I can say I am busy working my business for eight hours a day. But when I stop and really see where my time is going, it does not take long for me to notice when I go from working to scrolling on social media. All of a sudden, I am reading about where Kim Kardashian was vacationing last week and who broke up with who in Hollywood. Being on my phone or sitting at my computer for hours does not necessarily mean I am being productive or successful. For my business, productive work is about the amount of time I spend doing income-producing activities. Following up with leads, generating new contacts, selling products, etc. I hate to burst your bubble, but mine has had to be burst many times as I have had to a step back and do a self-evaluation. What are the things you are busy doing?

> **THE TRUTH:**
> It's okay—and necessary—to say no to some things.

We tend to feel guilty because we think the world will stop spinning if we don't shoulder another responsibility. But inevitably, we end up taking on too much. We must practice evaluating our priorities so that we can have time and energy to pursue our dreams.

SAY NO

When we begin pursuing our dream, we have to start paying attention to our capacity and capabilities in each season. Every season is different, and we must remember that. You may be capable of doing more in the spring because you have more time, your overall mood is better, you feel more energized, and the sun is out for longer. You shouldn't force yourself to keep up with all the same activities in the fall when all your kids are getting ready to go back to school and circumstances aren't the same. Evaluate what you need in each season. We also must pay attention to what our motivation is for each activity in which we participate. We should not do things out of guilt or obligation. This is another area where we need to live out of abundance and not scarcity. We will need to have clear priorities and make sure that our actions and activities align with those.

> **When we begin pursuing our dream, we have to start paying attention to our capacity and capabilities in each season.**

I had been putting my dreams on the back burner when I said yes to every opportunity that came my way. Even though I was trying to honor and show love to my kids and husband, I was giving them less than the full version of me by stretching myself too thin. I started to take stock of my priorities and realized that I am most filled up and most myself when I take time for myself and my dreams.

YOU CAN DO HARD THINGS

That next year, I took a break from MOPS, I stepped down from my leadership role in Junior League, I stopped running all the play-dates, but I still served on a committee in the league that I enjoyed. I did not volunteer to be room mom, although I signed up to bring something amazing for every party. (May I never repeat that end-of-year party fiasco again, dear Lord.) I was building a business from the ground up, which was quite time consuming, so I did have to say no to a lot of other things in that season. But those things I chose to say yes to? I made sure I wanted to do them. I was no longer just saying yes out of guilt or because I felt pressure. I was saying yes because it was on my heart to serve in that area or those things were going to help me get closer to accomplishing my dreams and goals. I was more intentional.

At my daughter's school the next year, instead of putting together last-minute party favors and crafting at midnight because I didn't have time to do it before, I was just picking up the cupcakes I had signed up to bring. I wasn't stressed, and I enjoyed just getting to be present with my daughter at her class party. I didn't spend a year stressed about all my Junior League meetings, leadership requirements, volunteer hours, and so on. I just helped with the Junior League Holiday Expo that I love, and that was it. And in all honesty, right now, I am no longer am active member of the League but a sustaining member. I pay dues because I love the cause, but I am not serving on any committee. Why? Because in this season with my three children and a business, I do not have the time. I am aware if I said yes to that, it would take away from another area I need to focus on.

I know the only way I was able to build my business so quickly and reach the top of my company in less than two years was because I removed a lot of other things from my plate. I want to reiterate I removed things I liked and enjoyed, but just for a season. Just because I said no to a lot of moms' nights out and even play dates for my kids at the beginning of my business does not mean I have to say no now. Just because I gave up all TV last summer while I was making time to write this book does not mean that I did not watch my favorite Christmas Hallmark movies in December. Please remember, seasons change, so just because you say no now does not mean you cannot jump back in at another time. I had to learn this all the hard way. I refuse to run around like a chicken with my head cut off anymore, doing everything half way because I can't say NO. Friend, you can say "no" or "not now" and not feel guilty about it. You are only one person, and I believe you can truly do anything you set your mind to. But I also know you cannot do everything.

To keep this in check, every so often I do an evaluation of my life and what I am doing. I get out a piece of paper and a pencil, and I start making a list. What are my responsibilities and duties? What are those things that are not optional like being a mom, wife, maybe caring for an elderly parent. Then there is your career. Do you work outside the home or in the home, and what are those duties? Keep your list going, and don't forget to write down your hobbies or things that are important to you. Working out, that book club, volunteering, church commitments, blogging, whatever it is that you love, and then get into all the "extra" stuff as well. As things come up and you are asked to do this or that, make sure you can say yes. Make sure it won't take too much away from another area that you need to focus on.

As you move through seasons, you might notice your dreams start to change. As this happens, what you say "yes" and "no" to will change. My dream was always to be a stay-at-home mom once I had children. I have loved, loved, loved my time doing that, and that is still a huge desire for me. But along the way, I also found out that I love helping people—especially women—learn to dream again. I became passionate about my business, and then I even became passionate about writing. So my dreams have shifted some. I want to be present with my time with my children, and I also want to be focused and intentional when I am growing my business and pursuing other new dreams the Lord has placed on my heart. It is okay for your dreams to change and evolve. For me, the key component is to periodically re-evaluate my schedule and see what all is on my plate. Then I have to make sure I have said yes to the right things that are most important to me and my dreams.

> **Make sure that you make the time to say yes to things that will help you get closer to your dreams.**

SAY NO

Make sure that you make the time to say yes to things that will help you get closer to your dreams. Don't buy into the lie that saying no to opportunities in order to follow your dreams is selfish and wrong. Following and living out your dreams makes you the fullest version of yourself! What part of being fully you is selfish? Taking time for yourself will mean saying no to other opportunities—but the opportunities that will come up for your dreams will make saying no easier over time.

If your dream is to be an author, start writing. If your dream is to run in a triathlon, start conditioning. If your dream is to have a cake shop, start baking in your spare time. If your dream is to be a nurse, start studying and enroll in school. Make the time for what is important to you and what sets your soul on fire. And like I always say, you may have to give up some of the good for the great, but I can promise it will be worth it.

YOU CAN DO HARD THINGS

REFLECTION:

Do you have too much on your plate right now?

What can you say no to that will free up time for you to pursue your dream?

Chapter 11

YOU CAN HAVE IT ALL

> **THE EXCUSE:**
> I can't ever have it all, so why try?

Being the mom, wife, business owner, and friend who goes after her dreams seems like you'd have to be Superwoman. I am definitely not Superwoman; I am barely holding my life together. Why would I add another thing—especially something as selfish as a dream—to my schedule?

I grew up with two loving parents. My dad adored me and my siblings. We were truly his world. But he was a workaholic. I think perhaps he worked so much so that he didn't have to think about everything he had endured during Vietnam. He lived with PTSD; he was one of the only ones from his platoon who made it home alive, so he saw and experienced a lot. My mom wanted to stay home with my brothers, sister, and me, but we needed the additional income. She had an in-home daycare. She was also responsible taxiing all of us to dance, gymnastics, karate, football, basketball, Little League baseball, swim team, track and field, piano lessons, violin lessons, drum lessons, Girl Scouts, theater. Between the four of us kids, we did it all, and it was on her to get us from place to place.

My dad worked and that was his thing. He gave it his all, and I would venture to say with all of the overtime he did, he probably worked an average of sixty hours a week. My mom gave her all to raise four kids plus run a full-time daycare with twelve other kids. As a result, their marriage wasn't a priority, not because they didn't love each other but because they didn't make time for it. My dad could have chosen to take one less overtime shift and instead go on a date with my mom, but that didn't happen.

All that to say, as busy and crazy as life is, I don't think the problem is not having the time. We are all operating by the same twenty-four-hour day. The problem has to be not making the time. When my dad passed away, my mom had a hard time coming to terms with the fact that the two of them didn't get the time together that she hoped for. She knew they were living these two separate lives, just co-existing. She held on to the thought, "One day, we will spend time together. When the kids are grown, when we retire by the water, that will be when we get our marriage back."

Last chapter, we talked about learning we can say no. This chapter, I want to address the excuse we make when it comes to thinking it's impossible to have a full, emotionally healthy life. There is a lot of talk about self-care and emotional health, but for many of us, a well-rounded routine and schedule focused on holistic emotional health and work/life balance sounds like a pipe dream. We're better off settling in some areas because otherwise we will end up heartbroken, right? It's not entirely unreasonable to make this excuse. In fact, I think majority of people's lives probably look more like what my parent's lives looked like. I look at my parents and see two people who were really trying to provide for their children and pay the bills, but ultimately, they neglected other parts of their life until it was too late. Reflecting on their life experiences drove me to question if I'm crazy for thinking all these dreams in my heart are remotely possible in my one little life. Does having a thriving business mean I can't be a good mom? Can I have a great marriage and raise my children? Am I allowed to have dreams and things I am passionate about and still be present with my family? Do I have to choose between self-care and having a social life? Is it possible to have all the things? And if I can't have all those things, is it even worth the effort to try?

During a season where I was all-consumed with work and reaching my goals, not only were my children suffering but so was my marriage. My husband was so incredibly supportive with my business. He wanted me to succeed and reach the top level of the company. He had a full-time corporate job, so he was gone all day. When John would come home, things were pure chaos. I was trying to keep up with the kids and my business, so when he walked in the door, I acted like he had been absent on vacation all day and now it was time for him to get to work and actually help out! I would give him his mile-long list of tasks I needed him to complete. This poor guy went from work to even more work. My attitude toward him and the long list that I would hand over was not necessary or beneficial for our marriage. Looking back, a hello and kiss would have been a much better greeting than passing off a child and saying, "It's your turn to change the diaper," and retreating as fast as I could to my room.

One night, I was scarfing down my dinner while staring at my phone, probably answering questions from my team. My goal was always to eat as fast as I could so we could clean up, quickly do the whole kid bedtime routine, and put the kids to bed. Once all that was out of the way, I could have some uninterrupted time to work. Thank God my girls were so young that they will not remember this season, because it was out of control and is not a time I am particularly proud of.

John looked at me that night as we sat around the table and he said, "Could we maybe have some blackout time during dinner?"

"What?" I responded.

He went on to say it would be nice if we could make dinner a time when we black out work, phone calls, emails, and just eat as a family. My heart sank. I got that sick feeling you get when the wind gets knocked out of you. All this man wanted was for me to put down my phone for twenty minutes to be present for dinner. He had been gone all day and just wanted to see my face and my eyes. Instead, he stared at my forehead because I had my face glued to my phone screen. For some reason, it seems to take an earth-shattering, rock-bottom moment for me to wake up and change. I realized not only was my face staring at my phone all dinner, but not much changed until I went to bed. I never ever turned off. John would usually go to bed, and I would stay up working until the wee hours of the morning. I realized we hadn't even had a conversation where I was focused and listening to him in months. Our marriage was more like a roommate situation.

From the night on, we began implementing "blackout" time, not just at dinner but in our life. To this day, I usually don't even take my phone with me into a restaurant and if I do, I leave it in my purse. Date nights with my husband, which we make an absolute priority, blackout time. Mornings with my kids, blackout time. When one of my girls wants to play a game of UNO or have me help with a craft, blackout time. If we are meeting friends for a playdate, blackout time. Family dinner, always always always, blackout time. Story time before bed, blackout time. Many evenings John and I decide to get in the hot tub or sit on the patio and talk, blackout time.

Blackout time didn't result in my business suffering. The opposite happened, actually. My business was more successful when I took time to put effort and thought into my relationships. Blackout time helped me realize the

> **You don't have to sacrifice everything to have the life you want.**

YOU CAN DO HARD THINGS

importance of making space and time for other priorities. You don't have to sacrifice everything to have the life you want. You can truly have it all. The secret is self-discipline and time management. There is so much time in the day to get what you want out of life. You just need to set boundaries and set specific times and days for activities, and in doing so, you will set yourself up for success.

> **THE TRUTH:**
> Having it all means being disciplined enough to set boundaries and schedules.

If you want to be Superwoman, my guess is Superwoman keeps a calendar, turns off the TV a little earlier, and has routines in place that line up with her priorities. You can have it all, you just have to be intentional and know what having it all means to you.

We know by now, we have to create some boundaries and structures in order to bring dreams to life. This, as we have said, means some of those extra things are going to have to go. But as you evaluate what you're saying no to, also evaluate what you're going to show up for. Don't forget to say yes to the things that propel you towards your dream. If you are quitting something you truly want to do and are passionate about pursuing, re-think it. Don't quit just for the sake of quitting. Just re-prioritize your time, tweak your schedule, look to see where your time is going.

If I can strive to be a rocking mom, great wife, good friend and successful business owner, why can't you? We all have the same twenty-four hours in a day. I do not believe the question is if you have the time; I think the question is what are you doing with your time. Where and when are you wasting time? Maybe you could scroll Instagram less and be present with your kids or spouse more. Maybe you could give up a Netflix show or two. (I mean, how many series do you really need to be watching all at once?) What if instead of spending so much time on Facebook, you decide to take some steps to pursue that dream in your heart or work that business you said you wanted to do. If you find yourself admiring someone and wondering how do she does it all, I bet you she is disciplined and makes good use of her twenty-four hours. So what are you doing with your twenty-four hours?

It is important for me to say that I believe in order to be successful—and I mean truly successful with something—you do have to go all in and work hard. But does going all in with one thing mean you neglect everything else? No! Hear me when I say, the problem is not going all in and giving your all to something. The problem comes when you let everything else go out the window. Last chapter, we talked about learning to say no. The balance here is that we must learn to say no to those extra things that don't align with the season we are in, but we must say yes to the most important things. It breaks my heart that my parents said yes to their work and to providing for our

YOU CAN DO HARD THINGS

family, but never fully said yes to their marriage. As you evaluate your time and priorities, decide right now what your list of important things are and then decide to do them all well.

***

In the direct sales industry, people join, they give it two weeks, and then they quit. It is mind-blowing when I look at the number of people who join my team and quit before ever giving it a shot. I have always found it strange how many people pay the ninety-nine dollars to begin and then throw in the towel without truly trying. They give, let's say, 20 percent of their effort, and then if they aren't making a million bucks their first month, they are done. They "tried," it didn't work, the company didn't work, the products didn't work. It's always everyone and anyone else's fault but theirs. If you want to know the truth, the real reason is usually that they didn't work. They did not give it their all; they did not jump all in. Maybe they only gave 20 percent effort because in the past, they'd had they given 100 percent and not succeeded. They would have been let down anyways, so they held back. Maybe they only gave 20 percent because they were skeptical or worried what others might think. I hear all the reasons and all the excuses. But what I do know is that the few people who go all in and hold nothing back and then stick to it . . . they win. They succeed. Everyone goes at different paces, but I have yet to see someone jump in feet first and give it their all consistently and not have results.

When I started my business, I went all in and there was no stopping me. In hindsight, I could have managed my time better. I would have made some changes, implemented a little (okay a lot) more blackout time, and I still could have had the same results by just shifting some things. But it did take that all-in hustle to have the success I did. After leading one of my company's top teams for the past five years, I have seen tons of other people do exactly what I did. They joined, they refused to quit, and they put in all, and I mean all, of their effort.

Every year, the CEOs of my company host a weekend retreat for a group of the top leaders in the company. What blows my mind every year is the diversity in this group of successful people. We're talking high school dropouts, people with their PhDs, college students, grandmas, teen moms, former professional athletes—the group is so diverse. But every year as I observe and connect with the top leaders, I notice one thing. There is one thing all these people have in common. There is one thing that took them from the starting point to building massive teams that bring in millions of dollars in sales each month. They are hard workers. They went all in, they let their obstacles and their excuses push them forward instead of stop them in their tracks. They decided to use whatever resources and opportunities available to work hard to thrive. It got hard, so they worked harder. People talked about them, so they worked harder. Team members quit, so they worked harder. They missed a promotion, so they worked harder. Their willingness to give it their all and not stop is what sets them apart. And I would guess that you would see these same attributes among all high performers in various fields.

As I gave so much of myself to my business, I then figured out how to give my all to every area of my life. My children when I am with them, my husband when we are spending time together or on a date, my business when it is work time. I learned to manage all this so that I could thrive in all areas, not just one. It is amazing that when I am focused and intentional in my designated work time, I do not feel guilty when it is time to be all in with my kids during mom time. I don't feel bad turning on a movie and watching it with my husband at night because I got my work done when I was supposed to and I spent quality time with my children when they were awake. What a dramatic change from what my days used to look like. At one time in my life, I neglected everything else but work. Other times, I put my dreams on the back burner and only focused on being a mom and wife, and that left me unfilled. I believe you can have it all if you are willing to be disciplined with the time you have.

Now I am not saying that I have figured this all out and mastered it perfectly. But I do know what it looks like to feel healthy in my life and in the way I am prioritizing my responsibilities. I also know what it looks like to be a complete mess. Every so often, I pause and take a step back and really evaluate all those areas of my life so I can see if and where I need to make some adjustments. On a recent weekend, John and I took our kids to the local farmers market. We walked in and my phone started to ding, I found myself in work mode, missing out on the first twenty minutes of the family outing. I soon realized that while I was there physically, I was not truly there. So, I shut my phone and showed up to really be present with my husband and children. After we left the market, I realized I didn't even get a good family photo because I was focused on spending good quality time with them without my phone in my hand, which is a pretty good thing if you ask me. Do I have it all figured out? No way, but I am always willing to make corrections and adjustments in my life when areas get out of whack.

John 10:10 says, "I came that they may have and enjoy life, and have it in abundance [to the full, till it overflows]" (AMP). The Lord intended for us to live a life of overflowing abundance in every area. This will mean self-discipline on our part. We must stay focused and keep our priorities as priorities. If we don't stay focused, then lines begin to blur, priorities shift without our conscious awareness of it, and our life begins to become chaotic and unfulfilling. In order to properly pour into relationships and priorities, we need to make taking care of ourselves a priority. How are we being filled spiritually, emotionally, physically? We must make sure we are being poured into in order for us to pour into others in a healthy way.

I want to show you what this has actually looked like in my life. On the following pages, there are two

YOU CAN DO HARD THINGS

dramatically different schedules: what my life used to look like and what it looks like now. As you read them, think about what your own schedule looks like. Make note of which one feels more similar to your own.

Identify your roles and the things you want to do and then make time to do each of them well. You can achieve your dream without giving up everything else. Yes, it takes discipline but I believe you can do it. If you need to come up with a strong why for each area, do it! And maybe it feels unusual to you, but make a schedule for yourself and see if it starts to make a difference as you pursue your dreams and fulfill your responsibilities across the various roles you hold in your life. Design a life you love, and be sure that you run it and it doesn't run you.

> **Design a life you love, and be sure that you run it and it doesn't run you.**

HAVE IT ALL

My Old Schedule

MORNING	Wake up when my kids wake me up crying (no self-development or discipline).
LATE AFTERNOON	Try to balance my kids and work at the same time, get distracted scrolling through social media.
DINNER	Rush through dinner while staring at my phone.
BEDTIME FOR KIDS	Hurry and get the kids to bed so I can work more.
EVENING	Work until I almost fall asleep.
BED TIME	No set bed time whatsoever.

YOU CAN DO HARD THINGS

My Current Schedule

MORNING	Wake up at 5:30 a.m. Have quiet time and journal until 6:30 a.m. List out responsibilities for the day.
LATE MORNING	At 6:30 a.m., get my kids ready for school. Listen to audiobook while I get ready for the day.
AFTERNOON	Work a few hours. When the kids get home, set aside intentional time with them.
DINNER	"Blackout time" to focus on John and our kids.
BEDTIME FOR KIDS	Intentional time for bedtime prayers and story time.
EVENING	Work on a project or hobby; spend time with spouse.
BEDTIME	Set a specific bedtime.

REFLECTION:

What are your roles? (mom, wife, friend, employee, boss, etc.)

In order to do well in all of these roles, you have to take care of yourself. How are you taking care of yourself? Physically, spiritually, emotionally?

Do you have a schedule you live by? Jot down some thoughts of some changes you might need to make in your day.

Chapter 12

YOU CAN SHOW UP

> **THE EXCUSE:**
> I'm so tired and don't have the energy to dream.

Life has knocked me down. I've experienced great pain and loss and I'm not sure how to move forward. I do not feel motivated. I do not know if I have it in me to dream or be ambitious.

One month after my husband and I got married, I was talking to my mom on the phone. I heard my dad say bye to my mom from over the phone as he walked out the door to go to a PTSD counseling appointment at the VA. That was the last time I ever heard his voice. At fifty-eight, my dad had a heart attack at the VA. He was in a one-room restroom and the door was locked, so no one knew he had a heart attack until late that night. I was twenty-two at the time.

I was really close to my dad. Even though he worked a lot when I was growing up and he wasn't always around, he still managed to express his love so well. He always called me princess my whole life, as if that was my name. I am pretty sure at six years old, I thought I was a real princess. His love language was gifts, so every week as a child, I knew to look in my top dresser drawer when I woke up because he would hide one of my favorite candy bars in there. My mom never liked candy in the house, so this was most definitely our secret. A few weeks before he died, he walked me down the aisle at my wedding—a moment that was very special to me then and even more treasured now. That was one of the last days I ever saw him.

Grief is indescribably hard to carry, and it never fully goes away. And everyone walks through their experiences of it so very differently. Walking through that loss at twenty-two years old as a newlywed was one of the hardest experiences of my life. My first year of marriage was hell. I was not sure if we were even going to make it. My family was turned upside down. My mom had to figure out life as a widow with my ten-year-old sister and fifteen-year-old brother still living at home. I watched firsthand how different people deal with loss. My little sister internalized it all and didn't want to talk about it. I had a brother who turned to drugs, and at one point, ended up homeless on the streets. My other brother was so consumed with guilt that he literally disappeared and didn't talk to my family for an entire year. I saw myself begin to feel angry and resent my husband because his family was so perfectly intact while mine seemed to be crumbling into a million pieces.

I definitely felt stuck, or maybe a better word is

paralyzed. My goal was just to get through each day without having a total breakdown. I was not thriving, I was not dreaming, I was just going through the motions. I put a lot of things on the back burner for a while. And that happens. But as some point, you have to decide if you are ready to show up again. I had to get myself together, to start working on my marriage and communicating my emotions to my spouse. I had to decide to start showing up again for my life as well as my dreams. After those foggy days of grief, I got back involved with our young adults ministry at church, I re-enrolled for my college classes so I could finish getting my degree, I started getting out of the house and re-connecting with friends. My dad would not want me to stay in a dark place; he would want me to get up and keep going. I'm not sure what emotional burdens you have shouldered in your life, but I have to take this space to say that you should never be scared or ashamed to seek professional help or counseling if you're walking through a season of grief.

It was only through God's strength that I found comfort, my heart softened, and I began to heal. Is it fair I lost my dad at twenty-two? Is it fair that my dad will never meet my children who I just know he would have adored? Is it fair my mom became a widow at just fifty years old? No, none of it is fair. But you know what? Life is not fair. Death, loss, and tragedy are going to happen. These things are often inevitable, and we cannot control them. But we can control how we react to the difficult seasons of our lives. And although I never "got over" the loss of my father, I was able to move forward, walk through the grief, and not let this pain keep me stuck. I have to choose to show up for the people around me and the things that God has called me to do.

Grief is a very important process, and I'm not saying that you can't grieve or be sad! Not at all! But at a certain point, which is different for everyone, you have to decide to look past the sadness in your heart and show up for yourself and the people around you. And I am not comparing my story to yours because I know there are many of you who have endured the unimaginable. We all have a different story that is so very personal to us. But regardless, holding onto grief, reopening wounds, reliving your most painful experiences, and maybe even blaming yourself for them will keep you stuck, unable to be present and move forward. We have to do the hard work of moving forward, not just for ourselves, but for others around us. The people around you who love you want to see you thriving; they want you present because that is how to live your best life.

> **We have to do the hard work of moving forward, not just for ourselves, but for others around us.**

SHOW UP

> **THE TRUTH:**
> We have one life to live, so it's time to decide what we are going to show up for.

Are we going to let life drift past us or are we going to show up and live each day even more present and ready to dream than the day before? How can we show up to be better wives, mothers, friends, and business owners? We first must remember that we are allowed to have dreams and pursue them!

In order to begin to truly show up for your life, you have to first realize you have one life to live. James 4:14 is pretty darn clear if you ask me. We are clearly told, "You don't know what will happen tomorrow. Your life is like a fog. You can see it for a short time, but then it goes away" (ERV). As we have gone through all these excuses we make for ourselves, one underlying thread is we think the excuses will go away someday, and then we can start doing what we actually hope to do. We think that the kids will grow up and the work will slow down. We think more time will come. Stop saying *someday* when someday is not promised. All you have is today, right now. Are you going to show up or just let the hours of the day pass by and hope things will be better tomorrow?

When we show up for ourselves, for our dreams, and for the people God has called us to, we will experience so much more healing from our pain than we ever thought imaginable. When we show up, we are choosing to not let our feelings and emotions rule us; we are choosing to not be selfish in how we respond to painful situations. We are choosing to process our emotions in a healthy way with people we trust. We don't have to hide or lie about how we feel; we just need to be honest about it. Showing up means fully being yourself—all your dreams, feelings, emotions, stories, pain, joy, gratitude. It means being fully present with yourself.

I'm not for a minute pretending showing up is easy. For me, grief would come in waves and hit me so unexpectedly at times. I would be doing great, and then a song would play, or something would happen that would make me want to pick up the phone and call my dad. It was hard, but I would try to find something to be grateful for in those moments. I would think about the twenty-two years I was blessed with an amazing father. I would think about how so many of my dad's character traits rubbed off on me and have shaped me into who I am. It never took the pain away, but it gave me a little bit of joy in the midst of the heartache.

> **When we show up for ourselves, for our dreams, and for the people God has called us to, we will experience so much more healing from our pain than we ever thought imaginable.**

Thirteen years later, I still get hit by grief. This past Christmas, there was a moment where all three of my kids were dancing to Christmas songs. My dad loved Christmas songs, especially ones by Elvis or Frank Sinatra. I couldn't help but wish my dad was here in this very moment to see them sing, laugh, and dance. I so badly wish he could have met them. My heart was heavy the rest of the day, and I had a hard time sleeping that night. I replayed the day he passed away as I laid in bed, and I wondered if there was any way it could have been prevented. He had been having chest pains leading up to his death. Should I have made a bigger deal about him going to the doctor? He didn't listen to my mom when she told him to go get things checked. What if he would have listened to me? But then I had to stop my mind, stop wandering down the never-ending road of "What Ifs," and say, "God, I still don't understand why. It doesn't make sense."

My dad passed away thirteen years ago, and his last Christmas here was the last Christmas my siblings and I were together. My family has never ever been the same. My brothers don't even talk to each other. I hate it, but I have to let go and trust God. I have to cling to the promise He gave me in Romans 8:28 that "we know that all things work together for good to them that love God . . ." (KJV). I want to carry on his legacy; I want to make him proud. My dad had learning disabilities growing up like me, and writing this book is something I can do for both of us. I find myself letting pain, hurt, and even disappointments fuel my fire and cause me to want to rise up stronger than before.

I don't always want to show up and do the work that life requires of me. The number of mornings where I was tempted to check out and just take a day off are too many to count. But for my kids, my husband, my team, and myself, I choose to show up because ultimately, I'm deeply grateful for this life. Showing up on bad days requires implementing practices of gratitude and awareness. Gratitude for what is currently in your hands, who you have around you, where you've been placed. Awareness for what you need in order to be present, awareness about the needs of the people around you, awareness of things to be grateful for.

One of the potential dangers of talking about dreams all the time is that it can maybe start to sound a little disconnected from the tougher realities of life, like grief and loss and financial struggle and marriage difficulties. But on the contrary, I have seen that deciding to go after our dreams for our life is often born out of these struggles. You may have some battle wounds, scrapes, and scars, but you've survived, my friend, so let's show the world what you've got. Let that hurt and pain be part of your story and testimony. Yes, it is easier to leave those dreams on the back burner, to not fight, to stay knocked down and remain broken. But what kind of life is that? It is not a John 10:10 "life-to-the-fullest" kind of life, and that's the life that I want. I know more junk is going to happen. I will walk through more loss, hurt, disappointment, and the list can go on. But I will still have a choice. I can stay there in brokenness, or I can take the shattered pieces, maybe even the dust that's left from the pieces, give them to God, and let him put them back together again. You are too strong to give up. You have been called to too much greatness to stay broken.

***

My mom talked for years about getting her real-estate license after my dad passed away. My mother is one of those people that strangers can instantly fall in love with. She has that bubbly personality. (Unless you mess with one of her kids, then I would say she is more like a ticking time bomb.) But most of the time, she is sweet as pie with a little Georgian drawl. She had all those qualities a great real estate agent should have. My mom took the first steps of getting her real estate license and took all of the preparatory classes after my father passed away. She was going to take her exam, but then she ended up moving to Texas to be closer to my family. Once she got to Texas, she had to retake her classes since the exam would be a bit different here, but she never got around to taking the final state exam for her actual license. I guess you could say life happened. She was a widow, still raising my younger sister who was just starting high school, she became a grandmother and was helping me a lot with my first baby. As a result, her real-estate

> **I can stay there in brokenness, or I can take the shattered pieces, maybe even the dust that's left from the pieces, give them to God, and let him put them back together again.**

dream went back on the back burner as she served and helped everyone else.

It is not always hurt or pain from a tragedy or bad experience that keeps us from showing up for ourselves or the dreams we have. Sometimes, we get too busy or just too complacent about where we are in life. Believe me, I know there are days when the thought of really taking a look at your dreams and figuring out how to pursue them seems so exhausting. And when you're tired, you don't even let your mind go there. Instead, you just let the days pass and you stay busy with everything else.

I mean, let's be honest, it isn't very hard to have a full plate, even if not one of the items on that plate is for you. So many tasks, roles, and excuses push our dreams to the back burner—that place in our heart and mind one we never use and often forget about. As we've gone through this journey of understanding the excuses we make for ourselves along the way, we're starting and ending in that same place. We don't think it's possible for these dreams to come true, or that it's not the right time, or that the things we are going through are too difficult to move beyond. And I really don't want those excuses to hold you back any longer. I want you to show up for your life. I want you to not get to the end and realize you were so "busy" scrolling through everyone else's lives that your life never really started.

What lies are you buying into that keeps you from showing up for yourself and your dream? What lie are you buying into that keeps you from taking that last exam,

SHOW UP

launching your business, or registering for classes? Maybe you have bought into the lie that there isn't enough time, things are fine how they are, and life is okay. It might be that you're weighed down by comparison, or you feel all alone, or you've said yes to too many things and the dream will have to wait. If you have a dream, then you deserve to see it through. It won't be easy, you may have to fight for it, but you deserve it. You have a responsibility to show up—right here, right now—for those dreams you have. It is time to stop thinking about them and wishing they would come true. And as matter of fact, some of you need to stop constantly talking yourself out of them. What if today was the day you decided to wake up and show up for your dreams?

***

Friends, we have examined all the excuses in our way to living the life of our dreams. We can name all those things that hold us back. But we know the truth: that excuses don't have the final word on our life. We can reframe our mindset. We can adjust our priorities. We can cultivate habits of hard work and hustle while also practicing rest and being present with the people that matter most to us. In all these pages, I genuinely hope you see the full spectrum of what it means to dream. Yes, it is painful and difficult at times. It sure would be easier to ignore the problem areas in our lives and keep making excuses. But the truths we've explored are more powerful than the lies we've believed for far too long.

In my journey as a wife, mother, friend, and business owner, holding on to these truths on my hardest days was vital to finding breakthrough for my dreams. And I really, truly, honestly believe that if you commit to planting these truths in your heart, you will see growth in so many areas of your life. As we come to a close, I want to remind you of all the truths I hope you take hold of after reading this book. I want you to print them out and tape them on your mirror. I want you to know them by memory and call them to mind when that dream feels out of reach. You can't keep your dreams on the back burner any longer because sister, the world needs what you have to offer. It's time to do something with what you've got.

YOU CAN START. To go after your dreams, you have to just start.

YOU CAN FIND YOUR WHY. You have to understand the "why" behind your dreams in order to work toward actualizing and achieving them. Whys help you identify your motivation and give you a reason to keep working toward your dream.

YOU CAN FAIL FORWARD. You can't let fear of failure stand in your way. Even if you fail, you will fail forward and will learn through the process.

YOU CAN HAVE VISION. Having vision and belief is never crazy. Vision is the only way that world-changing things are accomplished. Vision to see yourself actually accomplishing your dream can only lead to growth and prosperity. Don't sell yourself short.

YOU CAN WORK FOR IT. Achieving dreams takes action and discipline. You may not be a magical unicorn whose dreams come true overnight, but you can be a self-disciplined hard worker and achieve your goals.

YOU CAN RELEASE YOUR PAST. Your past is a part of you, but *hallelujah!*, it's not your present or your future. You must think forward and set your sights on what is ahead. Your past is just that: your past. It's time to learn from it and move on. It's not who you are anymore! You can use your experiences to lead others to freedom and healing. You are never disqualified from pursuing your dreams.

YOU CAN BE ENOUGH. Your "enoughness" is not measured up next to anyone else. You must adjust how you speak to yourself and find your worth not in others, but in God and the identity He's given you. You are enough and God has given you gifts and abilities to achieve your unique purpose on earth.

YOU CAN TUNE OUT THE CRITICS. Let your truth be louder than any other voice. Even Jesus had critics. Don't let critics stop you from pursuing your dream. Listen and trust yourself. Trust your intuition. Trust God's plan for your life. Don't let others shrink your dreams. Let your success speak for itself and silence their criticism, and find the voices that cheer you on.

YOU CAN FIND YOUR PEOPLE. You can't pursue your dreams alone. You must go after your dreams, and in order to do so, you must have support. There are women out there who will cheer you on and lift you up.

You can be a wife, mother, and business owner, and have wonderful friends!

YOU CAN HAVE IT ALL. Having it all means being disciplined enough to set boundaries and schedules. If you want to be Superwoman, my guess is Superwoman keeps a calendar, turns off the TV a little earlier, and has routines in place that line up with her priorities. You can have it all, you just have to be intentional and know what having it all means to you.

YOU CAN SHOW UP. You have one life to live, so it's time to decide what you are going to show up for. Are you going to let it drift past you or are you going to show up and live it each day? How can you show up to be better wife, mother, friend, and business owner? You first must remember that you are allowed to have dreams and pursue them!

YOU CAN DO HARD THINGS! See it. Believe it. Pray for it. Work for it.

SHOW UP

REFLECTION:

What are some things that you are grateful for?

How can you show up today?

Conclusion

YOU CAN DO HARD THINGS

> *"If there ever comes a time when the women of the world come together purely and simply . . . it will be a force such as the world has never known."*
>
> — MATTHEW ARNOLD

Not too long ago, I had that dream to write a book. And for a while, I let myself believe that I would never be able to see that goal come to life. But as I come to these final pages, I am again reminded—I can do hard things! This little book is such a testimony to what can happen when you ditch the excuses and start taking hold of truth. When that happens, the possibilities for what we can accomplish in our lives multiplies by thousands. Just like my multifaceted dreams as a kid, I want my current dreams to reflect that adventurous, limitless, curious, imaginative energy. We aren't too old or too logical for that! We just have to replace the excuses that keep us from our dreams with the truth that enables us to reach our full potential. We can return to that childlike belief that we can do and be anything. Because yes, we really can do hard things.

How? Take the daily steps to see your dreams become reality. It will be a difficult process, but what you create, build, and leave as your legacy will be so worth it. As a woman, you have been taught to shrink back and do what is required of you, but I really want you to set those expectations aside and think about yourself for a minute! Think about your dreams and what you could accomplish if you set your mind to it. We must persist in our pursuit of dreams—daily. To do hard things, we must cultivate rhythms of dreaming. I know I've mentioned quite a few key truths, but I want to leave you with one little phrase that is easy to remember and repeat to yourself. As I like to say: See it, Believe it, Pray for It, and Work for it. This is a pattern of thought we can return to each time a new dream enters our hearts!

> We just have to replace the excuses that keep us from our dreams with the truth that enables us to reach our full potential.

SEE IT. Visualize your dreams; know what you want to accomplish. Dream big and don't limit yourself. I have always believed that seeing that dream in your head is the first step to it actually happening! If you can dream it, then why can't it become a reality? I first saw and visualized every single dream that came to pass before it actually happened.

BELIEVE IT. Believe in yourself and what you can

CONCLUSION

achieve. Believe that you can reach your dream. The battlefield of the mind has always been my greatest obstacle. I know that if I truly believe my dream can come to pass, then there is no stopping me. I think something shifts when you actually believe that dream you have can come true. If you are struggling with belief, I challenge you to start praying that the Lord will increase your faith! Every time I set out to accomplish a new dream, I find myself praying that the God would give me the faith I need to believe it can happen.

PRAY FOR IT. Realize that you can't do it all in your own strength. You need God and people around you who can encourage you and support you. I will be the first to admit I am nothing without Him! When I operate out of my own abilities and my own strength, I fail every time. But when I rely on God and His power working through me, I know I can do anything. Don't go at it alone. Remember that you have a heavenly Father who birthed that dream in your heart for a reason, and that means that you do not have to try to accomplish it alone.

WORK FOR IT. Start taking practical, attainable steps toward your dreams. This is the one step so many people neglect to implement. What are the steps you have to take for that dream to come to fruition? Just start! Regardless of how things look or how you feel, you have to begin. Even if the battle with doubt continues in your mind, you have to make the choice to work for your dream. If you never take that first step, you will never reach the destination.

YOU CAN DO HARD THINGS

When you start implementing these four steps into your life, the excuses and lies will pop up trying to stop you, but now you can fight against them with the truth you know and the power you have. If any voice, including your own, tells you that you can't do something, then get stubborn and prove that voice wrong. Don't let your fear of failure, fear of rejection, or fear of criticism get in your way. If you allow the dream to expand and if you let yourself be fully invested, there won't be room for any of that fear.

People who pursue their dreams change the world and change life for the people around them. It may seem selfish to follow your dreams at the expense of some other things in your life, but it isn't! Doing something that utilizes the gifts that God gave you isn't selfish—it is purposeful. We need to start dreaming big and working hard so the women around us will follow suit. Imagine what the world would look like if every woman went after their dream in a big way. Imagine what the world would look like if women stopped letting people limit them, their abilities, and their dreams. That is the world I want to live in, and the best way of getting there is pursuing our own dreams! You can't preach what you don't practice.

I never in a million years thought pursing my dreams

> **If any voice, including your own, tells you that you can't do something, then get stubborn and prove that voice wrong.**

CONCLUSION

would impact so many others around me, but it has! I think one of my favorite things is when friends or even acquaintances from social media send me a message and say that me starting my business from home inspired them to do the same.

Every year my family makes dream boards like I mentioned before, and we always post those dream boards on social media. It has been so neat to get messages and have people tell me that they now do family dream boards because they watched my family do them year after year. See, pursuing your dreams goes way beyond what is visible to you, and who knows how far-reaching your dreams will be.

When I decided to start my business and really let myself dream big about what could happen, my life changed. I was audacious and thought: *Why not dream about going to the top of the company? Why not dream about being one of the Top 10 in the company out of hundreds of thousands? Why not just go for it?* I decided to see it, believe it, pray for it, and then work for it. For whatever reason, I really believed I could do it, and as a result, I actually really did it. Accomplishing that changed me. It gave me this massive belief that I really could do what I set out to do. So, I started setting goals every year and doing them. While not all have come to pass, many have! The old SheriLynn probably would have been too scared to dream of writing a book and then actually doing it, but the new me says, *Why not? Why can't I write a book? Why can't I write multiple?*

YOU CAN DO HARD THINGS

As you come to the close of this book, I hope you begin to put these things I've shared with you in action. Take the necessary, daily steps to start achieving your dreams—even the small starting steps are important. Surround yourself with people who encourage you and support your dreams. Let your own voice of truth and purpose speak louder than any criticism. Be yourself fully.

I want to encourage you to dream. Don't put limitations on yourself; don't let the world put limitations on you. And don't stop at dreaming. You were put on this world for a reason and there is a purpose only you can fulfill. Take those first small steps.

Why can't you do whatever it is that is on your heart? I mean it. Women have been accomplishing their dreams and shattering glass ceilings for centuries and centuries, so I think it is your turn. The time is now; you were created for such a time as this. I, for one, am cheering you on from the stands. You can dream big, and you can do hard things.

Acknowledgments

I have so many people to thank. I have to first thank my best friend, soulmate, ride or die, and better half, John. You are one of my life's greatest gifts, and I am so thankful for all your love, support, and patience (oh the patience it takes to live with me!). Thank you for the being the constant rock and support in my life. You always cheer me on, encourage me when I'm down, and push me to go after my dreams. I love you endlessly.

Mom, you are a warrior, and I have always admired your faith in the Lord through the different storms of life. Thank you for instilling a faith in me that did not return void. Oh, and thank you for fervently praying for me during some of my wild and crazy high school years I'm sure you wish you could forget.

Mark and Cindy, thank you for letting the Lord use you two to impact this world and teach an entire generation how to dream big.

Calen, I am so grateful the Lord brought you into our lives as not only a friend but someone who would walk with us through this process and ultimately lead us to the right people to make this dream a reality.

And a special thank you to Esther and The Fedd Agency for turning this dream of a book into a reality and for guiding and helping me every step of the way. Cheers to hopefully the first of many books to come.

Endnotes

1. Aspell, Nathan. "J.K Rowling's Explained Why She Didn't Use Her Real Name When Harry Potter Was Published & It's So Not Cool." Capital FM, July 11, 2017. https://www.capitalfm.com/news/jk-rowling-full-name/.

2. Zurawik, David. "From Sun Magazine: Oprah -- Built in Baltimore." baltimoresun.com, December 9, 2018. https://www.baltimoresun.com/entertainment/bs-xpm-2011-05-18-bs-sm-oprahs-baltimore-20110522-story.html.

3. Moss, Caroline. "Anna Wintour Thinks Everyone Should Be Fired Once." Business Insider. Business Insider, March 3, 2015. https://www.businessinsider.com/anna-wintour-thinks-everyone-should-be-fired-once-2015-3.

4. Gillett, Rachel. "How Walt Disney, Oprah Winfrey, and 19 Other Successful People Rebounded After Getting Fired." Inc.com. Inc., October 7, 2015. https://www.inc.com/business-insider/21-successful-people-who-rebounded-after-getting-fired.html.

5. *You've Got Mail.* Warner Brothers, 1998.

6   Coelho, Paolo. *The Alchemist*. New York: Harper Collins, 1988.

7   Meyer, Joyce. *Battlefield of the Mind: Winning the Battle in Your Mind*. New York, NY: Warner, 2002.

8   "Roger Bannister Runs First Four-Minute Mile." History.com. A&E Television Networks, February 9, 2010. https://www.history.com/this-day-in-history/first-four-minute-mile.

9   Morrissey, Mary. "The Power of Writing Down Your Goals and Dreams." HuffPost. HuffPost, December 7, 2017. https://www.huffpost.com/entry/the-power-of-writing-down_b_12002348.

10   Gladwell, Malcolm. *Outliers: Why Some People Succeed and Some Don't*. New York: Little Brown & Co., 2008.

11   Robbins, Mel. "How to Stop Screwing Yourself Over." TED. TEDxSF. https://www.ted.com/talks/mel_robbins_how_to_stop_screwing_yourself_over/transcript?language=en.

12   Martin, Emmie. "This Chart Shows How Much More Money Men Earn than Women in the U.S." CNBC. CNBC, July 29, 2019. https://www.cnbc.com/2019/07/29/how-much-more-money-men-earn-than-women-in-the-us.html.

13 Conley, Courtney. 2019. "The Number of Women Running Fortune 500 Companies Is at a Record High." CNBC. CNBC. May 16, 2019. https://www.cnbc.com/2019/05/16/the-number-of-women-running-fortune-500-companies-is-at-a-record-high.html.

14 Brown Brené. *Daring Greatly: How the Courage to Be Vulnerable Transforms the Way We Live, Love, Parent, and Lead.* London, England: Penguin Books Ltd, 2015.

15 Roosevelt, Thedore. "Citizenship in a Republic." Speech at the Sorbonne, Paris, April 23, 1910.

ABOUT THE AUTHOR

SheriLynn Alcala is a wife, mom of three, and entrepreneur. She currently leads a multimillion-dollar business and is passionate about empowering other women to rise up and pursue their dreams. Throughout her life, SheriLynn struggled with learning disabilities, battled an eating disorder, and walked through many challenges when she started her first business as a stay-at-home mom. Through these challenges, she learned how to ditch the excuses, regardless of what the situation looked like, and dream anyway. SheriLynn lives in Dallas, Texas with her family of five.

For more updates about
You Can Do Hard Things,
visit www.youcanthebook.com
or follow SheriLynn on Instagram:
@sherialcala

NOTES